A King For Portugal

A King For Portugal

THE MADRIGAL CONSPIRACY, 1594-95

MARY ELIZABETH BROOKS

———————

THE UNIVERSITY OF WISCONSIN PRESS

MADISON AND MILWAUKEE

1964

Published by
The University of Wisconsin Press
Madison and Milwaukee
MAILING ADDRESS: P.O. Box 1379, Madison, Wisconsin 53701
EDITORIAL OFFICES: 430 Sterling Court, Madison
Copyright © 1964 by the
Regents of the University of Wisconsin
Printed in the United States of America
by Kingsport Press, Inc., Kingsport, Tennessee
Library of Congress Catalog
Card Number 64-22233

CONTENTS

ILLUSTRATIONS

Following page 88

Sebastian I, King of Portugal
Letter of Doña Ana de Austria to Philip II
Doña Ana de Austria
Philip II, King of Spain
Sentence of Gabriel de Espinosa
Ruins of the convent at Madrigal de las Altas Torres
Anonymous letter received by Don Rodrigo de Santillán
Scribal account of Inés Cid's ratification with torture

A King For Portugal

INTRODUCTION

*E*very generation in every country produces its share of charlatans, frauds, and confidence men, but the number of clever impersonators, attempting an audacious deceit of far-reaching proportions, is very small. The history of the Iberian Peninsula offers one such case which, if it had been successful, would have shaken the political structure of the peninsula, occasioning the outbreak of armed conflict in which England and France in all likelihood would have joined. Although the plot failed and the conspirators were executed for treason against the Spanish Crown, the impostor himself has survived in literary form as the Pastry-maker of Madrigal, well-known to the reading public of Spanish-speaking countries, even outside of Spain.

On August 1, 1595, Gabriel de Espinosa, pastry-maker of the Spanish town of Madrigal de las Altas Torres, was executed for impersonating the deceased King of Portugal, Sebastian I. Although the Gabriel de Espinosa of history was recognized immediately by the authorities to be an impostor whose impersonation was given no serious consideration, his mysterious airs and equivocal answers in prison led many people to believe that he was someone other than just a humble pastry-maker. Shortly after his death an anonymous account of the incident was published, emphasizing the mysterious aspect of Espinosa's conduct, and the metamorphosis of the *pastelero* began. Spanish writers of the seventeenth, eighteenth, and nineteenth

3

centuries, who used the anonymous account as their only historical source, discarded some elements and embellished others until king and pastry-maker were at last fused into one imposing, legendary figure. The story related in literary works is either the arrest and execution of a pastry-maker who was masquerading as King Sebastian of Portugal, or the deliberate liquidation by Philip II of Spain of his royal nephew Sebastian, who had assumed the identity of a humble man. In this dual identity, as in the case of any clever impersonation, lies the attraction for author and reader alike. If Espinosa was nothing more than an impostor, his was a grandiose and audacious attempt to deceive the most powerful monarch of Europe by resuscitating the rash young Portuguese king, killed in battle fourteen years before. If he was Sebastian, now willing to assume again after a long period of self-inflicted penance his responsibilities as ruler of the country whose fortune he had so selfishly destroyed, he suffered an even greater tragedy when his true identity was denied him and he was branded, instead, impostor and traitor.

The impersonation attempted by the real Espinosa was a well-planned conspiracy which was a product of two principal elements, one political and the other ethnic. Without the peculiar combination of circumstances, Espinosa's role in history would have been impossible. On August 4, 1578, King Sebastian of Portugal died on the battlefield at Alcazarquivir and two years later the throne of Portugal was occupied by his uncle, Philip II of Spain. The loss of political autonomy was a bitter blow to the Portuguese people who had long feared Spain's domination, but they found cause for hope in the rumors that Sebastian still lived. No one had seen the young king killed, and it was said that he had returned secretly to Portugal with the fleet after the battle. During the next thirty years, four false Sebastians were imprisoned and sentenced by the Spanish authorities: two in Portugal, one in Spain, and one in Italy. Even after the time had elapsed when Sebastian might still be alive, the hope for his reappearance was maintained by the *sebastianistas* who identified Sebastian with the already existing tradition of a national messiah.

The complete story of the *Pastelero de Madrigal,* then, lies in both history and literature. In order to understand fully the role played by the real Gabriel de Espinosa, one must start with Sebastian, the young king whose place Espinosa hoped to fill, and the symbolic importance he had assumed in Portuguese minds. From the standpoint of history, Espinosa was only a product of historical circumstance, the victim of a political conspiracy, a nobody who had been tricked into believing that he could become a king; and, like the other false Sebastians, he paid dearly for his illusions. Unlike his companions, however, Espinosa succeeded in moving from the pages of history into those of Spanish literature. His refusal, even under torture, to reveal his true identity and his flair for the dramatic insured a continuing existence in Spanish letters. The *pastelero* has changed a great deal during the course of the centuries. His deeds, ambitions, hopes, and companions have been altered according to the whims of authors and the dictates of literary fashion. Nevertheless, as in the case of so many literary figures who were first historical persons, the mutations of literature can be traced back to some seed in history; and the historical account, replaced by the more popular literary versions, may prove to be more fascinating in its complexity and veracity than its artistic imitiations. The purpose of this work is to present the complete story of Gabriel de Espinosa, the Pastry-maker of Madrigal, in history and literature.

Chapter I, "The Quixotic King," is based largely on the accounts of contemporary chroniclers. Although it does not pretend to offer new discoveries in historical investigations—the noted Portuguese historian, Queirós Veloso, has devoted many years to work in this field—it does make available a succinct and reliable account of Sebastian's determined march to destruction of self and country. I have included a bibliographical essay, Appendix A, for those whose interest in the historical period may require further information. The presentation here of the Portuguese expedition to Africa necessarily is centered around the person of the young king and the traumatic effects of the defeat on the Portuguese people as a nation.

Chaper II, "The Wages of Folly," is a greatly-reduced summary of events which carried complex diplomatic and political ramifications not pertinent to the story of the *pastelero*. The point of interest here is the position of Dom António, Prior of Crato, as the people's champion against the ambitions of Philip II, since it was for Dom António's benefit that his faithful follower, Fray Miguel dos Santos, coached Gabriel de Espinosa in the role of King Sebastian.

The account of the conspiracy and its discovery by Spanish authorities is based on documents found in the Archivo General at Simancas, Spain, with the heading "Proceso contra Gabriel de Espinosa pastelero de Madrigal y fray Miguel de los Santos religioso agustino" (Sección del Estado, *legajos* 172–73). The *proceso* is composed of some four hundred documents, each given a folio number, but without order of chronology or subject. Since the majority of these documents are letters written by the investigating officers, reporting on their progress to Philip II or his various advisers, it was considered most fitting to present the conspiracy as it was slowly revealed through the reports. In this way one obtains a multi-sided view of the principal characters, the investigating officers as well as the prisoners, and many interesting glimpses of bureaucratic maneuvering, emotional attitudes, and local conditions.

The chapter on Sebastianism was included for two reasons: first, because no work dealing with one of the false Sebastians would be complete without some explanation of the persistent belief that Sebastian still lived; and second, because no account of this strange cult has been made available in English. In sixteenth-century Portugal there was widespread interest in revelations, the interpretation of dreams, prophecies, and particularly in the Judaic tradition of a national messiah. Although the Jews had been expelled from Portugal in 1507 by King Manuel, those who embraced Christianity in order to avoid expulsion (the "new Christians") were instrumental in keeping alive the interest in the appearance of a mysterious prince, called *O Encoberto* (the Hidden One), who would establish a millennial reign of peace and prosperity. The most popular interpreter of the *Encoberto* was a humble shoemaker, Gonçalo Anes, whose prophetic verses were circulated *sub rosa* even before Sebastian's birth. After the stunning defeat at Alcazarquivir, bringing economic ruin and the loss of political independence, a leader of messianic stature was needed to lead the country out of despair and interest in the prophetic verses increased. Although the four false Sebastians made no effort to identify themselves as the *Encoberto,* capitalizing rather on the persistent belief that the young king had escaped death on the battlefield, the fusion of the two currents was inevitable. After the execution of the last impostor in 1603, João de Castro, a Portuguese exile in Paris, wrote his discursive works proving that the national messiah, the long-awaited "Hidden One," was King Sebastian, who would return some day to fulfil the old prophecies.

I have chosen to leave all quotations in the original language, making no attempt to modernize, in the belief that the original words still preserve an emotional power and a subtlety of expression that would be sacrificed by textual tampering. For the benefit of those who do not read Spanish and Portuguese, Appendix B contains translations of all quotations other than those taken from literary works.

I wish to express my gratitude to Professors R. M. Duncan, Raymond R. MacCurdy, and Albert R. Lopes of the University of New Mexico for their constant encouragement and guidance and to Professor Antonio Sánchez-Barbudo of the University of Wisconsin. The basic research done in Spain and Portugal was made possible by a fellowship granted by the Institute of International Education, and preparation of the manuscript was supported in part by the Research Committee of the Graduate School of the University of Wisconsin from special funds voted by the State Legislature.

I

THE
QUIXOTIC
KING

Sebastian was the only child of
João, Crown Prince of Portugal, and Juana, sister of Philip II of
Spain. Prince João, always a sickly child and youth, died eighteen
days before the birth of his son on January 20, 1554; and Juana soon
returned to Castile, leaving her five-month-old son under the guard-
ianship of his grandparents, João III and Queen Catarina of Portugal. After the death of João III in 1557, Sebastian was crowned King
of Portugal with his grandmother serving as regent. Five years later
Queen Catarina persuaded her brother-in-law, Cardinal Henrique,
to assume the duties of regent so that she could spend the last days
of her life in a convent, free from the responsibilities of government.
Cardinal Henrique served in that capacity until Sebastian's fourteenth birthday, at which time the young king was given full
governing power.

Neither Queen Catarina nor Cardinal Henrique was able to control the high-spirited boy and the major part of his education was
left in the hands of Father Luis Gonçalves da Câmara, a Jesuit priest
who was recalled from Rome in 1560 to be Sebastian's tutor. In
1566 Father Luis Gonçalves became the king's confessor as well,
and as his influence over Sebastian increased, that of the queen
waned. Doña Catarina preferred that her grandson's tutor and
spiritual adviser be Castilian, like herself, but she submitted to the
wishes of Cardinal Henrique in the selection of Father Luis Gon-

çalves. The choice was an unfortunate one. The militant spirit of the Jesuits and the chivalric example of Ignatius Loyola encouraged Sebastian's recklessness and daring, closing his ears to any counsel of moderation and pointing the way to the quixotic crusade that ended on the bloody plain of Alcazarquivir.[1]

Although a few contemporary chroniclers deny it, the young king was born with physical defects and suffered from ill health.[2] The entire right side of his body was larger than the left side, but by rigorous training and ascetic living, he developed great strength in his arms and legs—strong muscles for taming horses and using the lance. He was of medium height, blond and blue-eyed with white, freckled skin, and his expression was severe and serious. From the age of twelve, Sebastian suffered from an unknown malady which increased in proportion to the amount of violent physical exercise in which he engaged. Fainting spells, nausea, dizziness, and other physical symptoms gave birth to the suspicion that the young king might not be able to produce offspring, but the rumor was never acknowledged officially.[3]

Although Sebastian's delicate health caused the Council of State to postpone the selection of his bride until a time when the young monarch might be old and strong enough to stand the rigors of marriage, it did not keep Sebastian from pursuing his training in horsemanship and the manipulation of arms. Hunting was his favorite pastime and the only pleasure permitted in the court. The strict religious training given him by Father Luis Gonçalves strengthened Sebastian's belief that he was destined to perform great deeds for God; hence, his primary concern was his personal physical and moral preparation as a soldier of Christ. He was well-educated and possessed an active imagination, but the documents which he drafted show great confusion of ideas and thinking.[4] The high-spirited and strong-willed boy grew to be a fanatical and egocentric man. The total lack of self-discipline—in a temperament which needed firm control—made Sebastian incapable of listening to advice. The slightest opposition to his own desires sent him into fits of rage. He abused the older nobles who counseled moderation and restraint, surrounding himself with a group of reckless young men who fed his megalomania with flattery.[5]

Sebastian's grandfather, João III, had abandoned various forts in North Africa, including Larache and Alcazarquivir. Although it was a prudent decision, the action was generally condemned in Portugal; and Sebastian yearned to regain the lost territory. With the glorious examples of earlier empire builders to inspire him, Sebastian began laying plans for the conquest of Africa and a holy crusade against the infidels. In 1571, he obtained permission from the Pope to reform the three military orders of Portugal—Santiago, Aviz, and Christ. An arrow, symbol of the martyrdom of Saint Sebastian, was added to their habits, and prospective members were required to have three years' military service in India or Africa before they were considered eligible for membership. Sebastian himself entered the Order of Christ, and in 1573 he obtained from Pope Gregory XIII one of the arrows which had killed Saint Sebastian.

The following year, Sebastian sent his uncle, Dom António, the Prior of Crato, to Tangier as governor with specific instructions to wage war against the shereef. Shortly after Dom António's departure, Sebastian notified Queen Catarina and Cardinal Henrique that he had decided to go to Africa himself. Nothing could dissuade him from his determination to lead troops into battle in person. Cardinal Henrique was appointed regent, and Sebastian set sail for Africa in August with a small force of badly armed men. In Tangier he removed Dom António from his post as governor because he had failed to take the offensive against the shereef. Sebastian rode into the country every day with a small band of soldiers in the hope of finding some Moors to fight, but with the exception of one small skirmish, his efforts were fruitless. The king's utter disregard for his own personal safety terrified the nobles who accompanied him, and the government officials in Portugal were frantic upon finding that the country was without king or heir. In November, tired of his unsuccessful games of hide-and-seek with the shereef's disappearing forces and fearing that Queen Catarina might carry out her threat to go to Africa to fetch her erring grandson, Sebastian returned to Lisbon.[6]

After his trip to Africa, the desire to return at the head of a large expeditionary force became an obsession with Sebastian. He needed only an excuse, no matter how weak, to force his will upon the nation, and that pretext soon appeared in the form of a plea for help from the deposed Shereef of Fez, Mulai Mohammed.

In 1573 Shereef Abdallah, lord of all Barbary, died, leaving his throne to his son Mohammed. The new shereef's right to the title was promptly challenged by his two uncles, Abd-el-Malek and Ahmed,[7] on the basis that Mohammed's mother was a Negro slave. With military assistance from the Sultan of Turkey, Malek declared himself King of Fez in 1575, forcing Mohammed to flee to Morocco. In spite of the fact that neither Mohammed nor his father had been friends of Portugal, and despite the opinion prevailing among Spanish and Portuguese nobles that Portugal should not participate in the Moors' family rivalries, Sebastian seized the opportunity to take an active hand in North African affairs by offering his support to the deposed shereef.

Sebastian's first move was to obtain papal permission for a crusade and to enlist the aid of his uncle, Philip II of Spain. His principal argument for supporting Mohammed was the aid given Abd-el-Malek by the Sultan of Turkey. Malek would make the North African ports available to the Turkish fleet, Sebastian said, from which base they could easily attack the Iberian Peninsula. Philip II did not believe that the Turkish threat was as grave as Sebastian painted it, nor did he think that any military action in Africa was wise. He was quite aware of his headstrong young nephew's dreams of glory and tendency toward impulsive, erratic action; consequently, Philip delayed arranging the conference requested by Sebastian until relations between the two countries were becoming quite strained as a result of Philip's reluctance.

The meeting of the two kings finally took place at the Monastery of Guadalupe in December of 1576. All conferences were attended by the Duke of Alba, as military adviser to Philip, and Cristóbal de Mora, who served as interpreter.[8] The atmosphere was one of great cordiality and mutual affection; nevertheless, all concessions were made by the King of Spain alone. It was evident that Sebastian was determined to carry out his plan in spite of political, military, and financial reasons to the contrary, and Philip found himself forced to promise some aid or risk the ill will of the entire Portuguese nation. The assistance agreed upon was 50 ships, 5,000 men, arms, and provisions. Sebastian had also requested the hand of Philip's daughter, Isabel Clara Eugenia, but he was persuaded to wait until some later date when the young princess reached an age more suitable for matrimony.

Delighted with the results of the Guadalupe meeting, Sebastian returned to Portugal and began the enormous task of raising money and recruiting men. Normal means of revenue were not sufficient; special taxes were levied and donations from the nobles were solicited. Although the majority of the nobles opposed the expedition, they did not dare to do so openly. Many were forced to pawn their estates in order to fill the demands of the king. Sebastian insisted on handling all arrangements personally. His inexperience, refusal to take advice, and complete lack of organization resulted in utter chaos. Sebastian spent most of his time in training himself for the hardships of the campaign through violent physical exercise, spending long hours in the saddle and sleeping in tents, while the recruiting officers attempted to meet a goal of 12,000 men. Theoretically, every man of military age was subject to induction, but since money was very scarce, the government permitted draftees to buy their release. Neither the king nor his expedition enjoyed much popular support, and any man who could obtain the amount necessary for release did so. As a result, the recruits were inexperienced soldiers going against their will, and their number mounted very slowly.

One of the conditions under which Philip II promised material aid was that the expeditionary force should be ready by August of 1577. Sebastian's lack of efficient organization and the popular feeling against forced induction made it impossible to meet this deadline, but Sebastian did not believe that Philip would withhold aid once he saw that the plans would continue whether Spain participated or not. Sebastian was mistaken. Philip had promised to furnish men and materials only because Sebastian's determination had made it impossible to refuse. Now that Sebastian had failed to carry out his part of the agreement, Philip was released from his. War had broken out again in Flanders, and Philip used this as an excuse.

In all fairness to Philip, it must be pointed out that he did everything possible to dissuade Sebastian from his project. Many historians, particularly the Portuguese, suggest that Philip deliberately withheld aid in hope that Sebastian would not return from Africa and that his death would open the way to the union of Spain and Portugal.[9] There is no doubt that Philip longed and worked for peninsular unity, and his refusal to release some of his most able commanders, particularly those experienced in open field fighting, made the Portuguese defeat all the more likely; however, Philip had been quite outspoken in his opposition to the plans for the African expedition from the beginning. He worked through the Spanish ambassador in Lisbon in a continued effort to convince Sebastian, first, of the dangers involved in the African venture, and later of the folly of accompanying the expedition in person.

Sebastian's determination to lead the army into battle, leaving Portugal without funds, ruler, or heir, was the gravest error of all, but no one could dissuade him. His grandmother, Queen Catarina, died in February, 1578, only a few days after being informed of her grandson's intentions of accompanying the expedition, and Cardinal Henrique's protests only enraged Sebastian. At Henrique's request, the Senate (*câmara*) of Lisbon informed the king that the people did not approve of his going to Africa in person, and Sebastian's refusal to heed their advice caused anonymous notes, usually in verse, to appear in the palaces, pointing out the risks involved in his plans.[10] Sebastian, irritated by the display of public opposition, accused Henrique of stirring up the people against him. It was probably this ill feeling which kept Sebastian from appointing

Henrique regent during his absence, although Sebastian pretended that Henrique had refused to accept the post.[11] There is ample evidence that Sebastian could have attained his stated goals—wiping out any threat of Turkish attack from North African bases and retaking Larache—by negotiation, but the desire to defeat in the field the great African warrior, Abd-el-Malek, had become Sebastian's *idée fixe,* a compulsion that closed his ears to reason and blinded him to any facts that did not support his own opinions.[12]

Preparations for the expedition were drawing to a speedy close. Five governors were appointed to rule the country in the king's name during his absence, and Cardinal Henrique was named Sebastian's successor. In view of the cardinal's advanced age and absence of offspring, the Senate of Lisbon requested that Sebastian name a successor for his uncle as well; however, Sebastian refused to do so. He was so convinced of his own invincibility that he could not acknowledge the possibility of being killed in battle: thus, the matter of his successor's successor seemed too remote a matter to warrant attention.

By June, 1578, Lisbon had taken on the appearance of a huge military parade ground. Sebastian's confident spirits and conviction that Abd-el-Malek would not dare fight were contagious, and many nobles began to look upon the expedition as a gay excursion. Although few of them had relished the idea of joining the expedition at first, as soon as Sebastian announced his intention of leading the army in person, the Portuguese nobles were eager for the opportunity of fighting with their king. In spite of austerity laws forbidding sumptuous displays of servants, jewels, and equipment, each one tried to surpass the others in the lavishness of his entourage.[13] The noise and confusion arising from Sebastian's characteristic lack of organization was further heightened by frequent fights between the Portuguese soldiers and some 6,400 foreign troops who were to accompany the expedition. The Prince of Orange had sent 2,800 Walloons, Dutch, and Germans (many of whom were Protestants), and the Pope furnished 600 Italians under the command of the English adventurer, Thomas Stucley. Although Philip II had not permitted the recruiting of troops in Spain, some 3,000 Castilians volunteered. Eight hundred vessels were anchored in the harbor at Lisbon, waiting to transport these fighting men, plus 9,000 Portuguese, baggage, and supplies, to North Africa.[14]

On June 24 Sebastian boarded the royal galley and the fleet set sail. The king was accompanied by Juan de Silva, Spanish ambassador in Lisbon, who was acting as the personal representative of Philip II.[15] Although Sebastian was never a popular monarch and the country was already feeling the strain of the economic burden imposed by the expedition, the crowd cheered loudly as the armada set sail. The burst of enthusiasm, a result of momentary contagion, was short-lived. Too many of the recruits had been forced to go against their will, and their families' joy quickly changed to tears.[16] Only the *aventureiros,* a regiment of 1400 nobles who could not afford to buy the equipment necessary to qualify as *cavaleiros,* were genuinely happy to embark. This group, the major part of whom had seen service in other campaigns, was composed entirely of volunteers. Like Sebastian, the *aventureiros* believed that the campaign would be gay and glorious adventure, and it was said that each man's baggage contained a guitar—ample evidence of their carefree spirits.

After brief stops at Lagos and Cádiz for rendezvous with additional forces, the fleet divided at Gibraltar. The main fleet proceeded to anchor within sight of Arzila and waited while Sebastian took a small force to Tangier to meet the deposed shereef, Mohammed. Mohammed and Sebastian then went on to Arzila by sea, and the entire fleet disembarked together.

The army camped on the beach near Arzila, waiting for the arrival of supplies from the Algarve. Although Sebastian's pretext for coming to Africa was the capture of the port of Larache, he preferred to land at Arzila and march overland to Larache instead of attacking it by sea. The decision to march by land was a serious error. The time spent in Arzila waiting for supplies gave Abd-el-Malek the time he needed to assemble a huge army, and the Portuguese army was greatly debilitated by the long march over rough terrain. Sebastian, however, had good reason to believe that Abd-el-Malek did not want to meet the Portuguese army on the battlefield. The Portuguese enjoyed the reputation among the Moors of being fierce warriors, and Malek feared that his own followers would desert to Mohammed at the first sign of defeat. Furthermore, Malek's health was in a precarious state, and he was willing to give up a reasonable amount of coastal territory to Sebastian in return for peace. The only certain way, therefore, of forcing Malek to give battle was to march inland and attack Larache from behind.[17]

Another incident which evinces Sebastian's vehement desire to engage in personal combat with the shereef's forces occurred while the army was camped at Arzila. A large band of enemy horsemen approached on a scouting mission. A group of Portuguese rode out to engage them, and as the Moors withdrew rapidly, Sebastian and a small group of nobles rode after them for a great distance. The king's party was unable to overtake the enemy, but Sebastian's reckless pursuit without proper protection gave the more prudent members of his council ample cause for worry.

Sebastian was not only heedless concerning his own personal safety, he was equally imprudent about the vulnerability of the men who followed him. He refused to accredit any information regarding the strength of the forces being marshaled by Abd-el-Malek, and he failed to acknowledge the fact that the majority of his own infantrymen were raw recruits without any training or experience. One night an Italian sentry, failing to recognize the officer who was making the rounds, fired his arquebus. It was interpreted as a signal of attack, and in the panic which resulted, many soldiers deserted and fled to Tangier. No discipline was possible while Sebastian closed his ears to the advice of the older and more experienced men. He insisted on being the sole authority, the only person with the power to make decisions and give orders; consequently, his personal lack of organization and self-discipline was reflected in the conduct of the expeditionary force as a whole.

At last the long-awaited supplies arrived and the army prepared to begin the march inland on July 29. The eighteen days wasted at Arzila had permitted Abd-el-Malek to gather a force of some 30,000 men and to move them to Alcazarquivir.[18] Through information obtained from scouting parties and spies, he knew the exact size, conditions, and equipment of Sebastian's army. He had learned that the expedition contained less than 2,000 horsemen, many of whom were young nobles in their early teens,[19] and that the majority of the foot soldiers were unseasoned troops. But, most important, he knew that these soldiers were led by a young, inexperienced, and wilful king who rejected the counsel of those who accompanied him.

One of the experienced Spanish infantry captains whose services Sebastian had been very eager to obtain was Francisco de Aldana. Sebastian had written frequently to Philip II through the spring of 1578 requesting that Aldana be allowed to accompany him,[20] but Philip withheld permission until the last moment. Aldana and 500 Castilian soldiers reached Arzila two days after the army had started the march inland and would have missed the battle completely if Sebastian had not sent fifty horsemen back to Arzila to escort them to his encampment.

The army continued its exhausting march, plagued by the heat, the lack of food, and harassing raids at night on the baggage trains, until they approached the Mocazim River. Thus far the route to Larache and Alcazarquivir was one and the same; but at this point it was necessary to decide which course of action to follow, to cross the river and march on Alcazarquivir, or turn toward the coast and Larache. Until this time there had been no definite word of Abd-el-Malek's army, and most of Sebastian's council was in favor of going on to Larache where the fleet awaited with provisions. If this route had been followed, the Portuguese army could have reached Larache without danger of attack.[21] However, that same day a band of the shereef's horsemen were sighted near the Christian camp and news of the position of Malek's army reached Sebastian. His eagerness to vanquish the renowned warrior, Abd-el-Malek, overcame all counsel for prudence, and Sebastian's *amour-propre* would not permit a withdrawal which might be interpreted as a cowardly retreat. The precarious state of Malek's health was also known in the Christian camp. Mohammed urged Sebastian to wait until his uncle died, believing that the chieftains would accept him as shereef, but Sebastian refused. There would be little glory in defeating a dead man. Sebastian ordered the expeditionary force to ford the river and march toward Alcazarquivir.

On the morning of August 4, Sebastian drew up his forces in battle formation and advanced toward Malek's army which was waiting on a plain some fifteen kilometers from the town of Alcazarquivir. The formation taken by Sebastian's forces was roughly in the form of a square with baggage trains and noncombatants in the center. Francisco de Aldana was in charge of the infantry and Sebastian himself commanded the cavalry.[22]

When Abd-el-Malek saw that the Christian army was moving forward to attack, he also prepared for battle. His illness did not permit him to lead the army in person, so he directed his captains from a tent near the battlefield. The Moorish army was in a crescent-shaped formation with the infantry in the center and cavalry units on either end, thereby being mobile enough to surround the enemy. Realizing that he was near death, Malek named his younger brother, Ahmed, heir to the throne and gave him command of part of the army.

The first to open fire was the Moorish artillery. This caused a certain amount of panic in the Christian forces. Sebastian had specified that the order for attack would come from him alone; and since the king forgot to give the proper commands, his army suffered the first blow without knowing what to do. Sebastian, still failing to command a general attack, led his group of cavalry in a charge against the enemy. The *aventureiros* under Cristóvão de Távora also moved into action and the groups of foreign soldiers followed suit. These groups fought well and effectively, but there was no coordination of activity. Because Sebastian had failed to move his army as a whole, entire sections stood motionless, waiting for orders, until they were cut down by the Moorish cavalry.

If the Christian forces had been given adequate leadership that day, they might have succeeded in routing Malek's army in spite of being greatly outnumbered. Contemporary chroniclers point out one instance where the tide of battle could have changed if the opportunity had been recognized and seized. The fierce attack initiated by the *aventureiros* and foreign troops broke the line held by the Moorish *andaluces* who fled in panic.[23] Mulai Ahmed, believing that all was lost, was among those who ran, returning only after the battle was over.[24] When he saw this serious situation, Mulai Malek tried to mount his horse in an effort to rally his forces, but the physical exertion and emotional strain were greater than his weak body could bear. He fell dead from his horse and was carried into his tent. The death of the shereef was kept from his followers, and orders were still issued in his name. If the *aventureiros,* who reached a spot very near Malek's tent, had succeeded in finding his body and making his death known, there is little doubt that the battle would have ended in a Portuguese victory. This was prevented, however, by an event which did seem almost providential. A voice rang out, "Volta! Volta!" The front line of *aventureiros* stopped in confusion at the command. The Moors attacked furiously, and the *aventureiros* were pushed back. The ill-timed order had been given by an officer calling for the soldiers to come to the rescue of another officer who had been wounded.

The Christian army was surrounded and its artillery was captured. Isolated cells of resistance still fought on bravely, but there was no co-ordination of effort. All was confusion and the carnage was horrible. Leitam de Andrada, who fought with the *aventureiros,* gives one of the most graphic descriptions:

De maneira que de huns, & outros ficou aquillo por aly tè onde chegamos cuberto de mortos, homẽs, & cavallos, emtanto, que difficultosamente se podia por aly entrar a cavalo, depois: & tãto o sangue que em partes me dava quasi pello artelho. E tudo gritos, & lamentos, mortos em cima de vivos, & vivos de mortos, todos feitos pedaços, Christãos & Mouros abraçados, chorando & morrendo, huns sobre a artelharia, outros braços & tripas arrastrando, debaixo de cavallos & encima espedaçados, & tudo muyto mais do que ja vos posso dizer, porque apperta commigo a dor, na lembrança do que passei.* (p. 185)

---

*Translations of starred passages may be found in Appendix B.

Sebastian and a small group of nobles who were trying to protect him continued to fight desperately. The king had had three horses killed under him and had mounted the fourth. As the defeat grew worse, the nobles with Sebastian tried to persuade him to surrender before he was killed; but he refused, throwing himself again and again into the thickest parts of the fighting. The king was so heedless of his own safety and the confusion was so great that the horsemen who were accompanying him had difficulty in keeping up with him. They could only try to follow the royal banner.

The exact circumstances of Sebastian's death are not known since none of the survivors saw the king killed. The accounts given by the chroniclers present three versions, varying in detail, but agreeing on the fact that Sebastian was killed during the battle.

According to Mendonça (p. 48), Sebastian and a small group of nobles were so surrounded by Moors that one of the Portuguese nobles tried to negotiate a surrender. The arrogant demands of the Moors enraged Sebastian who rushed once more into the thick of the battle. He was not seen alive again.[25]

The accounts of Fray Luis Nieto (Ch. xii), Conestagio (pp. 36–37), and San Román (pp. 160–62) are practically identical. When Sebastian and his little group of horsemen tried to surrender under a white flag, the Moors fell on them and killed them. Either the Moors did not understand the attempt to surrender or they were so eager to take the royal prisoner that they inadvertently killed him. Conestagio and San Román further explain that Sebastian was not properly protected because the nobles mistook the banner of Duarte de Meneses for that of the king. Sebastian's standard-bearer was killed and the nobles, who were trying to rally around the royal standard, followed the wrong one.[26]

In the version given by Fray Bernardo da Cruz (Chs. lxviii and lxix), Luis de Brito, the king's standard-bearer, was fighting beside Sebastian against a group of Moors who were trying to take them prisoners. Brito and the royal banner were captured, and Brito last saw Sebastian moving away along the edge of the battlefield without anyone in sight who might stop him. The spot where Sebastian was seen by Brito, the last to see the king alive, was quite far from the place where his body was found; therefore, no one really knows how he met his death. Some conjecture that he was captured and killed by mistake. Others believe that when he was captured and ordered to undress, he resisted so violently that he was killed. Sebastian was extremely modest and would not allow even his closest servants to see his bare feet.[27]

Even before Sebastian's death, the Christian army was thoroughly defeated. The Moors were busy wiping out the small, isolated spots of resistance which remained, escorting droves of prisoners away from the battlefield, and pillaging the dead. The battle lasted only a few hours, but during that brief time half of the Christian fighting force died and less than 100 persons managed to escape and make their way to Arzila or Tangier. The rest—more than 15,000 counting noncombatants—were captured and held for ransom. Three kings died that day: Abd-el-Malek succumbed to his lingering illness; Sebastian died in the battle; and Mulai Mohammed was drowned while attempting to cross the Mocazim River. Portugal suffered a blow from which she never fully recovered. The cost of equipping the expedition and ransoming prisoners overburdened the nation's economy, and the death of her young king led to the loss of her liberty as an independent nation.

Fortunately for Portugal, Mulai Ahmed, the new shereef, decided not to follow up the victory at Alcazarquivir with an attack on Arzila and Tangier. Perhaps, as many chroniclers suggest, it was because he feared and respected Philip II of Spain. Ahmed's conduct in the handling of Sebastian's body was most cavalier, and he refused to accept ransom either for the young king's body or the person of Juan de Silva, Philip's ambassador, who was a captive.

The body of the unfortunate young King of Portugal was found on the battlefield by his *ajuda de câmara,* Sebastião de Resende, and was carried to the Moorish camp where the captive Portuguese nobles confirmed Resende's identification. When discovered, Sebastian's body was completely nude and showed seven wounds; nevertheless, the nobles present were certain that it was the body of

their king.[28] Ahmed ordered that the corpse be taken to Alcazarquivir for proper burial until the time that its return could be negotiated. Belchior do Amaral was selected to accompany the king's
body to Alcazarquivir, after which he was to notify the coastal
cities under Portuguese rule that they were in no danger of attack
and to send official word to Portugal about the battle and about
arrangements for the ransoming of captives. Amaral reached Arzila
on August 11 to find that the Portuguese fleet had already started
back to Portugal with the few survivors who had managed to
escape from the battle. He then went on to Tangier where there
was a squadron of ships waiting to pick up any additional survivors. The squadron commander carried to Cardinal Henrique
Amaral's letter with full details of the battle and the official notification of Sebastian's death. Amaral then returned to captivity as he
had promised.

The first definite news of the defeat to reach Lisbon was brought
by the returning armada under Diogo de Sousa; however, the few
survivors of the battle who came with the fleet did not know of the
king's death. Reports were confused and contradictory. Grief and
panic were widespread. As soon as the fleet arrived, Cardinal Henrique went to Lisbon and, on August 17, made public the word that
the expeditionary force had been defeated. On August 24 the squadron arrived with the letter from Belchior do Amaral saying that he
had buried Sebastian. Funeral services were held on August 27,
and Henrique was crowned the following day.[29]

The task of ransoming captives was indeed a great one. Portugal
was already on the verge of bankruptcy, and there was not a noble
family in the entire country which did not have one or more of its
members in the hands of the shereef. In the opinion of Cristóbal de
Mora, representative of Philip II in Lisbon, the Portuguese were
much more disturbed by the vast sums of money they would have
to raise than by the death of their young king. On August 26, Mora
wrote to the King of Spain: "...si hasta aquí deseaban velle vivo
no era por lo que le amaban, sino por verse libres de los inconvenientes que les podian resultar de su muerte."*[30] The bulk of

the money raised came from jewels and clothing which were sold in Africa, and package deals were negotiated for the ransoming of groups of nobles held in various cities. A year after the battle—October, 1579—the release was effected of the last group held in Fez. Although the common soldier did not fare as well as the nobles, thousands of them were also ransomed.

In the meantime, Philip II had requested the ransoming of his nephew's body through Andrea Corzo, a Genoese merchant who acted as his agent. Mulai Ahmed refused to accept the money and, as a favor to the King of Spain, promptly issued orders for the release of Sebastian's corpse along with Juan de Silva, Philip's ambassador who was captured during the battle. The king's body was exhumed and taken from Alcazarquivir to Ceuta where it was turned over to Fray Roque de Espíritu Santo, *comissário* of the Trinitarian Order. Sebastian was buried again in Ceuta, lying there until 1582 when Philip II, then Philip I of Portugal, had him moved to Lisbon for burial in the Monastery of Belém.[31]

II

THE
WAGES
OF
FOLLY

$\mathcal{A}$t the time that he ascended to the throne of Portugal, Dom Henrique, the cardinal king, was sixty-seven years old and tubercular. Cristóbal de Mora described Henrique's coronation as a "triste espectáculo," attended by a small number of people, "todos viejos y llorosos y el rey mas que todos."[*1] Sebastian had been an only child and his great-uncle, Henrique, being a prelate of the Church, had no offspring. Who, then, was the legitimate successor to Henrique? Three principal contenders pled their cases to Henrique in the hope that he would support their claim to the throne of Portugal when the *Córtes* was called in April, 1579. There were other claimants, but only the cases of Philip of Spain, the Duchess of Bragança, and Dom António were considered strong enough for consideration.

The most powerful of the three was Philip II of Spain who, through his mother Isabel, was the grandson of Manuel O Afortunado. As soon as the news of the Battle of Alcazarquivir reached Spain, Philip sent Cristóbal de Mora to Lisbon with the express mission of obtaining the support of Cardinal Henrique and the Portuguese nobles. Mora was Portuguese by birth and had performed many delicate missions in Portugal for Philip in the past. This time his job was even more difficult; he was to go to Lisbon under the pretext of offering condolences and helping to ransom captives, but the real purpose was to bribe anyone who could aid Philip's cause.

*Translations of starred passages may be found in Appendix B.

Mora reported his progress in secret correspondence carried on through Philip's secretary, Antonio Pérez.[2]

Another grandchild of King Manuel was Catarina, Duchess of Bragança, daughter of Prince Duarte. Her principal supporter was Cardinal Henrique himself. The loss of Portuguese autonomy, which would result from Philip's ascent to the Portuguese throne, was odious to Henrique; however, he realized that if he named Catarina (or her young son) as his heir, Philip would try to take Portugal by force. The country, already impoverished by the ransoming of prisoners, could not sustain a war against the powerful King of Spain.[3] As far as Henrique was concerned, the choice lay between the Duchess of Bragança and Philip II. At no time did he give serious consideration to the claim of Dom António despite the fact that Dom António was the choice of the people.

There was a long history of conflict between António and his uncle Henrique. Dom António was the illegitimate son of Prince Luis de Beja, brother of Henrique and João III, and Violante Gomes, a converted Jewess. Born in 1531, António entered the clergy to please his father and uncle; but after his father's death in 1555, he refused to complete the vows for the priesthood despite Henrique's insistence that he be ordained. Dom António's temperament was far more suited to the life of a gentleman and knight than it was to the Church. He was in constant difficulties with Cardinal Henrique and Queen Catarina about financial matters as well as his personal conduct which was not befitting a clergyman, and his attempts to obtain a papal release from his vows were a source of additional friction. By 1566 the family squabble had reached such proportions that Philip II sent Cristóbal de Mora to Lisbon for the express purpose of mediating some kind of agreement. Mora failed to obtain complete reconciliation between António and Henrique, but he did arrange for Dom António to receive a pension augmenting the small rents he received as Prior of Crato. Friction continued, and only after Sebastian became king did Dom António again join court circles. In 1574 he obtained dispensation from major vows so that he could enter the Order of Malta and fight against the infidels.

He accompanied the expedition to Africa as a member of the group of *aventureiros,* was taken prisoner, and returned to Lisbon on October 12, 1578.

Henrique's enmity toward António was so great that he seized the first possible opportunity to make António ineligible for consideration as his heir, and then he carried on a determined and systematic persecution of António and his followers. Although he permitted António to present a formal claim as pretender to the throne during the meeting of the *Côrtes* in April, 1579, Henrique had already requested papal permission to be the sole judge of António's legitimacy. In August, Henrique rejected António's claim that Prince Luis and Violante Gomes were secretly married and issued orders for the imprisonment of António as well as the witnesses who testified to his legitimacy. António appealed to the Pope, who had never authorized Cardinal Henrique's position as judge, but Henrique countered by declaring António denaturalized. Dom António was forced to flee to Spain where he had friends who would hide and protect him. The question of his legitimacy was never settled. In the turmoil which followed Henrique's death, António did not press the matter and it was eventually dropped.[4]

For a while Henrique had hopes of solving the problem of succession in another way. During the fall of 1578 increasing pressure from the Council of State, nobles, and representatives of civic governments was exerted on King Henrique to request papal dispensation from his ecclesiastical vows and to marry. In January, 1579, Henrique informed the Council of State of his willingness to request dispensation, and letters were sent to Rome through the papal nuncio in Lisbon. Philip II, however, was already working through the Spanish ambassador in the Vatican in an effort to block the dispensation, if and when it should be made. Pope Gregory XIII, torn between offending the King of Spain or the King of Portugal, postponed making any commitments, hoping that Henrique's age and ill health should settle the matter. And so it did. In June Henrique's health deteriorated rapidly, and the cardinal king gave up all hope of completing his marriage plans. The special legation which was to present the formal request for papal dispensation never left Lisbon.[5]

The pressures exerted on Henrique by Philip II were indeed great. Philip knew through his representative in Lisbon, Cristóbal de Mora, that Henrique favored the Duchess of Bragança, and he was also cognizant of the popular support given to the cause of Dom António. Philip understood, as well, the dilemma which Henrique faced—the decision between the odious union of Portugal with Spain if he named Philip his heir and the war with Spain which was sure to come if the House of Bragança ascended to the throne— and all Philip's efforts went into forcing Henrique to come to some decision before he died. If Cardinal Henrique should die without naming an heir, the popular elements supporting the Prior of Crato might make the invasion a costly one; and Philip preferred to get the crown of Portugal without using force. Cristóbal de Mora had done his job well and each day more Portuguese were giving their support to the Spanish cause in return for money or promises of future favors. During the meeting of the *Côrtes* in the early summer of 1579, Henrique appointed five governors who were to rule the country if he should die before a successor were chosen. Of the five, only one was openly against Philip's claim. Of the remaining four, one had already received money from Mora and three had accepted letters promising favors.[6]

By the fall of 1579, Henrique had all but given up the struggle against Philip; still, he hoped for some miracle which would remove from him the responsibility of choosing between war and loss of national independence. He tried to hold Philip at bay by declaring that he could not come to any agreement with Spain without the full consent of the Duchess of Bragança, the nobles, and the people. Another meeting of the *Côrtes* was called in January, 1580. Philip was confident of support among the nobles and clergy, but he anticipated trouble with the assembly of the people's representatives in Santarém. The problem of Dom António's legitimacy was still unsettled, and his popularity with this group was great. Philip's message, requesting that he be recognized as Henrique's heir, was presented to the Santarém assembly and debate was still in progress when Cardinal Henrique, the last king of the House of Aviz, died. Since Henrique's will contained no mention of an heir, the government passed into the hands of the five governors until the time that the *Côrtes* could select his successor.

No one mourned Henrique's death. His delaying tactics had offended many and pleased none. He was old and hesitant when Portugal needed a strong, resolute leader who could conciliate the warring factions within the country. He was struggling to preserve national independence; yet his hatred for Dom António, his failure to support the Duchess of Bragança, and his reluctance to offend Philip of Spain by curtailing the activities of Spanish agents, all made the preservation of that independence impossible.[7] The population as a whole was too exhausted to react to any crisis. The plague in Lisbon (which forced Henrique to move the court to Almeirim in June, 1579) was spreading to other cities, and the great number of victims further reduced a population which was already too small to carry on the agricultural activities necessary to feed the nation.[8] The expense of the expedition to Africa and the ransoming of captives had drained the country of its meager wealth. It was impossible to equip an army which could withstand the invasion force being prepared by Philip II.

The *Côrtes* in session at the time of Henrique's death adjourned without reaching any agreement. The representatives of the nobles and the clergy were not adverse to accepting Philip II, but the assembly in Santarém representing the people refused to give in. The five governors appealed to Philip for more time to call another meeting of the *Côrtes*. Tired of constant delays, Philip gave Portugal until June 8 to accept him by legal process. If not, the invasion force being assembled at Badajoz under the command of the Duke of Alba would take by force what was rightfully his.

When Dom António learned of his uncle's death, he came out of hiding and went to Santarém where the branch of the *Côrtes* representing the people was still in session. In this group lay António's greatest support; therefore, when the Spanish invasion became imminent, feeling grew there in favor of Dom António as the defender of Portuguese independence. On June 19, António was acclaimed in Santarém the rightful ruler of Portugal, and four days later he entered Lisbon without opposition. The governors fled to Setúbal, calling on local governments to accept Philip II and condemning the actions of Dom António as rebellion against the lawful government.[9]

The Spanish army moved across the border into Portugal on July 27, 1580. Towns and castles were surrendered without resistance and even Setúbal, where popular feeling ran high against Spain, fell without bloodshed. The rapid advance of the Spanish forces was viewed with alarm in Lisbon where Dom António was making feverish preparations for the defense of the city. Conditions there could scarcely have been worse: the soldiers—a poorly armed mob—were completely lacking in discipline and experience; there were no trained officers; and it was necessary to strip churches and monasteries of valuables to bolster the treasury. The Spanish army, advancing from the south, was transported by sea to Cascais on the north side of the wide estuary of the Tagus River. From Cascais, the Duke of Alba advanced slowly toward Lisbon, leaving each fort behind him well equipped. On August 25 the Spanish forces attacked Alcântara where Dom António had prepared to make his stand. After a brief but spirited encounter, the Portuguese forces were overwhelmed, and Dom António fled north to Coimbra.

Although the occupation of Lisbon was a decisive victory for Philip II, Dom António's escape was a great disappointment. With all of southern Portugal in enemy hands, António could only move northward with Spanish troops in close pursuit. The Prior of Crato made another attempt to defend Oporto against the invading forces, but it, too, fell. In spite of the price on his head offered by Philip, António stayed in Portugal almost seven months after the seizure of Oporto, moving from house to house or from monastery to monastery, protected and hidden by friends. At last, in May, 1581, he succeeded in crossing the border into France.

Philip II, accompanied by the royal family, entered Portugal in December, 1580. From Elvas he sent out letters calling for a meeting of the Portuguese *Côrtes*. Since Lisbon was still suffering from the plague, the *Côrtes* assembled a few months later in Tomar and on April 16, Philip II was crowned Philip I of Portugal. The new king stayed in Lisbon for almost two years. At the end of that time he returned to Spain, leaving his nephew, Cardinal-Archduke Alberto de Austria, in Lisbon as governor.[10]

The only remaining area of resistance to Philip's domination was in the Azores. Their government had recognized Dom António shortly after his entry into Lisbon, and even after the Spanish had occupied the mainland of Portugal, the Island of Terceira refused to accept Philip's sovereignty. The Spanish governor was expelled and a squadron of ships, sent from Lisbon to subjugate the area, was defeated by the spirited islanders. This loyalty to Dom António was a great asset in his appeals for aid to the courts of England and France.

England and France had shown early interest in the Portuguese succession. If Philip II succeeded in uniting the entire Iberian Peninsula under one ruler, it would make him a powerful and dangerous adversary. In the summer of 1579, the representative of Queen Elizabeth offered to Cardinal Henrique England's support in resisting any invasion by Spanish forces, and, at the same time, official representatives of England and France visited Dom António and the Duchess of Bragança. Elizabeth was particularly interested in the Duchess of Bragança and tried to negotiate an agreement with Henry III of France to support her claim to the Portuguese throne, but Henry was too busy with internal religious struggles. After Henrique's death both Dom António and the Braganças appealed to England and France for aid. Elizabeth urged the two claimants to reach some agreement so that a united front could offer some resistance to Spain; however, the Braganças refused to deal with the bastard branch of the family. Elizabeth's interest in the duchess waned as she became increasingly aware of the duke's indecision and lack of courage,[11] and the reluctance of Henry III to produce material aid kept the Queen of England from taking any action.

Henry's support was verbal only. In 1579 his agent had urged Dom António to lead a popular uprising after Henrique's death, yet when António was fighting the Spanish army, no help was sent from France.

António's courage and the popular support which he enjoyed made him increasingly attractive in the eyes of England and France, and both countries offered him political asylum after he was forced to flee Portugal. In view of the continued resistance of the Azores against Spain, the idea of equipping an expedition was looked upon with favor by some members of the English court,[12] but Elizabeth still rejected open conflict with Philip II. Some hundreds of Englishmen, however, went to France where Dom António was negotiating with Catherine de Medici. The price Dom António finally agreed upon was high. If the expedition against the Azores succeeded, Brazil would go to France.

On June 16, 1582, five ships set sail from France toward the Azores. Philip II, not unaware of Dom António's activities in the French court, was preparing naval forces in Lisbon and Seville to meet the attack. The two armadas met off the Island of São Miguel on July 26, and after a five-hour battle the French forces were defeated. The celebrations on Terceira, motivated by the arrival of António the day before the battle, were interrupted by the sad news of the defeat. In November António returned to France to enlist additional aid, but in spite of the reinforcements sent by Catherine de Medici, the Spanish armada succeeded in occupying Terceira on June 27, 1583. After three years of continued resistance, the last portions of Portuguese territory recognized the sovereignty of Spain.

The Prior of Crato would not abandon his protests against the Spanish invasion of Portugal. For six years he haunted the courts of England and France, living in poverty and moving from place to place to escape the agents Philip sent to assassinate him. The failure of the Azorean expedition had discouraged any additional aid, and Elizabeth of England was reluctant to open hostilities against Spain until the abortive attempt of the Invincible Armada to invade English shores gave her an excuse for retaliatory action. In April, 1589, an English fleet of twenty ships under the command of Sir Francis Drake sailed from Plymouth. Dom António accompanied Drake in the flagship. After sacking the Spanish port of La Coruña, the expedition landed on Portuguese soil at Peniche and started toward Lisbon. Dom António and his English allies had expected to receive help from the Prior of Crato's sympathizers in Portugal, but popular support failed to materialize. The rigors of martial law imposed in Lisbon and the imprisonment of those who were known to favor António's cause terrified all who otherwise might have joined him. The English force, lacking artillery and weakened by disease, soon abandoned the siege of Lisbon and returned to England.

While the failure of this second expedition eliminated the probability of further foreign aid, António did not desist in his demands. In 1590 he returned to France where he continued negotiations with Henry III and Henry IV until his death on August 26, 1595. The Prior of Crato is usually described as an irresponsible, undependable, and incapable demagogue, an opportunist who failed to win anyone's support because he tried to negotiate with everyone.[13] The eminent modern historian, Queirós Veloso, however, contends that Dom António's rightful place in Portuguese history is that of the symbol of Portuguese independence.[14] He describes the Prior of Crato as "valente, insinuante, generoso, duma grande cortesia de maneiras, qualidades admiráveis para inspirar simpatias, manter amizades sólidas, criar dedicações profundas."*[15] If he did engage in a certain amount of double-dealing before Henrique's death, he did so not for personal gain, but for the good of Portugal. It would have been much easier to give in to Philip II; but António risked his life, lost his fortune, and endured many years of hardship rather than be false to the ideal of Portuguese independence.

The entire picture of the union of Spain and Portugal is not a pretty one, and it is small wonder that contemporary chroniclers attributed the decay and fall of the Portuguese nation to divine punishment. A decadent aristocracy, too pusillanimous to oppose the plans of its megalomaniac monarch, accompanied him on the suicidal march to Alcazarquivir, then accepted the bribes of an alien state in wholesale betrayal of the nation. The people, usually a reliable mirror of the moral fiber of a country, succumbed to mass hysteria after the debacle at Alcazarquivir, resorting to witchcraft and superstition in their frantic search for orientation. National chaos made impossible any resistance to Spain's determined imperialism and discouraged the foreign aid which would have materialized if Dom António and the Duchess of Bragança had joined forces. One can scarcely envy Philip the prize he won with corruption, plotting, and bloodshed.

III

THE
LEGEND
OF A
BIRTH

*T*he loss of Portuguese autonomy was considered to be a direct result of the Battle of Alcazarquivir. All the ills which befell the unfortunate nation were traced back to the mutilated body of the young king found on the battlefield. If Sebastian had not insisted on the senseless African venture, if he had not led the army in person, if he had first provided the country with an heir, if he had not been killed, the union of Spain and Portugal could not have been effected. At least, so thought the Portuguese people. The indecision of Cardinal Henrique, the betrayal of the aristocracy, the uncompromising attitude of the Braganças, the apathy of the people, the skilful subversion by the Spanish agents—all these factors were disregarded. The national phobia of Portugal had become a reality; Portugal was swallowed up by Castile. The easiest explanation for this situation, which had developed in the short time of three years, was the disastrous expedition to Africa; nevertheless, the same blind loyalty which kept the nobles from obstructing Sebastian's march to certain destruction also prevented the country, after the battle, from laying the responsibility where it belonged, on the shoulders of the young king. Instead, the general belief was that Portugal's defeat was the will of God, divine punishment for the sins of the nation. Some chroniclers defend Sebastian as a monarch and as a person; others condemn him as a fanatical, irrational despot; but all indicate that he and his expedition to Africa were the instruments used by the Almighty to humble the proud Portuguese.[1]

According to Biblical tradition, before God punishes the wicked, He gives ample warning signs of His wrath so that the culprit has an opportunity to repent and alter his offensive conduct. Thus, accounts of heavenly indications of approaching disaster went hand in hand with the theory that the Portuguese defeat at Alcazarquivir was the will of God. All phenomona which were reported to precede Sebastian's death appear in chronicles written after the Battle of Alcazarquivir when there was an attempt made to explain the defeat; however, it is rather surprising that they should show up in the very earliest ones. With the exceptions of Jerónimo de Mendonça and Fray Luis Nieto,[2] all contemporary chroniclers and eyewitnesses point out the warning signs to support their belief that the defeat was divine punishment. These phenomena cannot be considered as products of Sebastianism, the belief in a national messiah based on the prophetic verses of Gonçalo Anes and applied to Sebastian. They are evidences of the same psychological patterns which nurtured *sebastianismo,* but their purpose is quite distinct. The *sebastianistas* tried to prove that Sebastian would return to Portugal in the role of a national messiah, whereas the chroniclers tried to show that his death and the ensuing misfortunes were part of a divine plan for punishment.

The most common reference to an evil omen is that concerning a large comet which appeared over Portugal in November, 1577. It was interpreted by some people as a sign of disaster, indicating the death of an important person; however, others preferred to look upon it as propitious. Its long tail resembled a whip which moved from Portugal to Africa, and in court circles it was interpreted as a signal for attack (a play on the Portuguese words for comet, *cometa,* and the command form of the verb "attack," *acometa*). Fray Bernardo da Cruz and Fray Bernardo Britto say that groups of armed men were seen in the sky at the same time.[3]

The appearance of other ghostly figures was reported, as well. Shortly before Sebastian's birth his mother was said to see groups of phantoms, Moors by some accounts, moving in and out of her bed-room, and the ghost of João III later appeared in an Augustinian monastery of Lisbon to express his disapproval of the African expedition.[4]

An interesting story about the royal banner appears in the chronicle attributed to Cruz (Ch. lxxv). The day the flag was blessed in the Lisbon Cathedral, it was placed on the pole upside down so that the figure of Jesus Christ was pointing head downward. On the day of the battle at Alcazarquivir, all efforts to unfurl the banner failed; it stayed tightly wrapped around the pole.

Many other supernatural phenomena were reported as if they were historical fact: Cardinal Henrique was served a swordfish for dinner that was clearly marked on one side with a cross and on the other with the year 1578; Sebastian heard songs of warning through the palace windows; as the royal galley raised its anchor to sail from Lisbon, it brought up the cadaver of a man; and the day of the battle a few drops of blood rained in Tangier, where battle noises could be plainly heard.

It is difficult for any country to accept castigation, even by the hand of God, without hope of reprieve. The Christian God is a merciful one, and the Portuguese could not believe that their punishment would be carried out without some opportunity for salvation. Defeat at the hands of the Moors was something to be accepted with resignation, but not the death of the heirless young monarch. Portugal was not ready to believe that Sebastian was dead. The first confused and contradictory reports of the battle brought to Portugal by the fleet spread through the country rapidly; and when the letter from Belchior do Amaral arrived, saying that he had buried the king in Africa, many refused to believe it. They had heard that Sebastian returned to Portugal with the fleet, and they were much more eager to believe that rumor than the announcement of his death. According to Cristóbal de Mora, even Cardinal Henrique was loath to accept the information contained in Amaral's letter:

... [Henrique] empezó á ejercitar su gobierno, dando siempre muestras de que no tenia por cierta la muerte del rey. Y sobre este caso habia tan diferentes y diversas opiniones, que hombres muy honrados afirmaban estar el rey vivo y en este reino, y daban testigos de cuando le habian visto. Y aunque es ordinaria la facilidad del vulgo en dar crédito a cosas semejantes, en esta provincia predomina mas esta facilidad que en todas las del mundo.*[5]

Although the fact of Sebastian's death was recognized officially, the belief that he still lived persisted. No one had seen him die. Former favorites of Sebastian, who did not enjoy equal favor with Henrique, supported the belief that the body buried at Alcazarquivir was not Sebastian's until Henrique was obliged to conduct investigations against those who were spreading such rumors.[6]

In spite of Cristóbal de Mora's opinion that these rumors were based on nothing but the overactive Portuguese imagination,[7] the belief that Sebastian had returned to Portugal with the fleet had its beginning in an episode which took place in Arzila the night after the Battle of Alcazarquivir. A small group of men, three or four, knocked at the gates of Arzila late that night. The sentries refused to open the gates, fearing an attack by the Moors, until they were told that King Sebastian was one of the group who sought admittance. The gates were flung open with great joy and torches were lighted. One of the men, wrapped in his cloak so that his face could not be seen, was treated with extreme respect by the others, and it was assumed that he was the king. The news was carried to the fleet, still anchored at Arzila. The next day when Diogo da Fonseca, a court magistrate (*corregedor da côrte*), and Captain Pero de Mesquita came to pay their respects, they found that the muffled stranger was a young noble who had played the part of the king in order to enter the city. Fonseca and Mesquita decided to keep the young man's identity a secret for fear that the people, when they learned of the deceit, would take his punishment into their own hands; and they allowed him and his companions to return in secrecy to Portugal with the fleet. Although Fonseca and Mesquita denied publicly that the young man was Sebastian, the false news had already spread.

*Translations of starred passages may be found in Appendix B.

Their failure to expose his identity added strength to the belief that the king sailed with the fleet.[8]

The conviction that Sebastian still lived was particularly widespread in the Azores. As long as there was some hope that Dom António, Prior of Crato, would triumph over Philip II of Spain in the struggle for the Portuguese crown, the islanders accepted and supported António. After the Spaniards succeeded in occupying the Azores in 1583, the belief that Sebastian was still alive spread with renewed credence; and the people prayed for two kings, António and Sebastian. A carpenter of the Island of São Miguel prophesied that King Sebastian would return to that island on March 10. On the day specified, a large ship passed within sight of the island; and although it continued on its way without stopping, the people insisted that they had seen Sebastian, his favorite, Cristóvão de Távora, and Mulai Mohammed standing on the deck. The monks at Saint Francis supported the belief that Sebastian was hidden in the monastery by ordering silken bed clothes and silver plates, feigning secrecy, and stating in sermons that there were two natural kings, not one.[9]

The people's refusal to accept Sebastian's death was motivated by the Spanish occupation. If the king were still alive, the gravest problem—the long-feared loss of national independence to Spain—would cease to exist. After the Battle of Alcazarquivir, the cult of *sebastianismo* was born of patriotism; however, one must go back to ethnologic, cultural, and religious conditions which existed even before the birth of Sebastian to explain the persistence and strength of the belief in his immortality. The Portuguese phenomenon of *sebastianismo* would have been impossible without the Celtic traditions of superstition and legend and the Judaic search for the Messiah.[10]

The revival of popular superstitions always accompanies social upheaval, and in Portugal the outbreak of war or epidemic brought forth new legislation forbidding the use of spells, fortunes, and other practices of occult nature. In the sixteenth century, both occurrences were frequent. The epidemic of 1569 was called the *peste grande* because of the great number of victims—estimated between 40,000 and 80,000.[11] Ten years later the plague in Lisbon forced Cardinal Henrique to move the court to Almeirim, and in 1581 similar conditions caused the coronation of Philip II to be held at Tomar. The disastrous African expedition, climaxing the political decline of Portugal, brought forth a reaction of mass hysteria, not only in the lower classes but among many nobles as well. Teófilo Braga reproduces a letter written in 1578 which describes Lisbon after news arrived of the defeat at Alcazarquivir: "É para chorar e acabar de pasmar da louquice d'esta terra. Haver n'ella donas ilustres e de qualidade com tão larga licença como tomaram, na desolação de andar no modo das romarias, e na invenção com que pedem a Deus vida e liberdade dos maridos e filhos captivos, porque não ha devoção defeza que não façam, nem feiticeria que não busquem, para lhes dizer o que vae em Africa" (*O Povo portuguez,* II, 169).*

The shock produced by the Battle of Alcazarquivir and Sebastian's death was even more violent than might have been expected because many Portuguese had hoped to find in Sebastian the fulfilment of their dreams for a national messiah who would lead the nation to new heights of prosperity and power. The only child of an only child, Sebastian was *O Desejado,* the one whose birth was eagerly anticipated, the one who might fulfil the prophecies of Gonçalo Anes, called *O Bandarra.*[12]

The ancestry of Gonçalo Anes is not known and little biographical data can be obtained from the Inquisition *proceso* drawn up against him in 1541.[13] A shoemaker of humble birth, he knew how to read and write; and his great knowledge of the Holy Scriptures caused his Biblical explanations, particularly those concerning prophecies, to be received with respect and awe. Bandarra's prophetic verses, called *trovas,* caused great excitement among those of Hebrew blood (called "new Christians" after their compulsory conversion to avoid expulsion in 1507), being first circulated orally and later in written copies. One copy fell into the hands of the Inquisition, and Bandarra was tried for Judaism. He made a public recantation, promising not to read or write anything having to do with Holy Scripture in the future, and the *trovas* were forbidden by the Inquisition. This public recognition increased Bandarra's fame, and interest in his *trovas* soon spread to "old Christians" (those without the taint of Jewish ancestry).

Although Bandarra was the first to give expression to the hope for a national savior, his *trovas* merely gave form to messianic elements which already existed in Portuguese culture. For that reason, they were accepted, circulated, and preserved long after his death. The Portuguese people were familiar with the Celtic legends of Merlin and King Arthur which were circulated by troubadours in the fourteenth century, and the Jewish prophecies of the Messiah were preserved by the new Christians of Judaic background.[14] Gonçalo Anes, the shoemaker from Trancoso, composed verses which combined elements of both traditions, couched in Biblical language and prophesying the coming of the Hidden One, *O Encoberto,* a prince who would establish the Utopian *quinto império,* a universal monarchy under Portuguese rule. The symbol of the *Encoberto* came from Spanish prophetic texts which circulated around 1520, attributed to Saint Isidore of Seville.

After the Battle of Alcazarquivir, interest revived in the *trovas* of Bandarra. The nationalistic party which opposed the claim of Philip II to the Portuguese crown began to use the prophecies, applying them to the return of Sebastian who was identified as the *Encoberto.* This new interpretation spread so rapidly that the Index of 1581 again forbade the reading of the *trovas.*[15] The desire for national independence had to find some outlet; and since there was no hope to be found in the Portuguese leaders who handed the country over to Spain, the people turned to the memory of the young king who became the personification of the courage and strength which had made Portugal a world empire in the past and which would again make her a great nation. While he lived, Sebastian was not a popular monarch; nevertheless, after the ill-fated expedition of 1578 and the misfortunes that followed, love of king fused with love of subjugated country in the minds of the people, making Sebastian the symbol of Portuguese freedom. Martyrdom and misfortune gave the young king a saintly aura befitting one who was predestined to be the savior of his people. This new interpretation of the old prophetic *trovas* is known as *sebastianismo,* a cult which was to survive through the early nineteenth century and which, according to some Portuguese, still exists today.

For the first thirty years following the Battle of Alcazarquivir, *sebastianismo* had strong ties with reality. There was no actual proof that Sebastian had been killed, and people looked for his return from Africa. During this period four men stepped forward to fill the gap left by Sebastian's death—two in Portugal, one in Spain, and one in Italy—but none succeeded in his role as the *Encoberto.* Portugal was waiting for the return of the same blond king who sailed to Africa, and no substitute would do. There were still too many people alive who had known Sebastian and who were not deceived by the impostors. Yet, Sebastian's return was desired so earnestly that the people were willing to accept each pretender as Sebastian until he was unmasked as a fraud. Only after his execution did they acknowledge the deceit and start searching for another who would be, in reality, the resuscitated king.[16]

The first man to take advantage of the belief that Sebastian still lived appeared in a deserted monastery near the Spanish border in 1584.[17] He was a dark-complexioned, gay-spirited young man, the son of a poor potter of Alcobaça, who had been living in Lisbon in 1578 when an epidemic of the plague forced him to enter a Carmelite monastery. After being expelled from the monastery because of his irrepressible temperament, he donned a hermit's frock and wandered from one place to the next until the summer of 1584 when he settled at Penamacor. He was visited by pious people in the vicinity and soon collected a following. The young man pretended to know a little Arabic, relating fantastic tales about the Battle of Alcazarquivir and entertaining his friends by dancing, singing, and playing the guitar. Soon the rumor spread that he was King Sebastian who was undergoing seven years' penance for losing the battle. Although he did not say that he was the king, he encouraged the dissemination of that belief by assuming regal and mysterious airs; and with the help of two ambitious accomplices, known as Cristóvão de Távora and the Bishop of Guarda,[18] he formed governmental councils of War and State. His fame reached Lisbon, and subsequent investigation showed that the people believed him to be King Sebastian. He was promptly arrested and a troop of Castilian soldiers escorted him to Lisbon, bare-headed and exposed to public view so that it could be plainly seen that he bore no resemblance to the dead king. The young man, known only as the *Rei de Penamacor,* never revealed his name; however, he defended himself with such wit that Cardinal-Archduke Alberto spared his life.[19] His two accomplices were sent to the gallows; and the young hermit served as a galley slave until 1588, escaping when his ship, which sailed with the Invincible Armada, was wrecked off the coast of France.

The activities of the second Portuguese impostor were more ambitious in scope and showed indications of a carefully formed plan rather than a spontaneous capitalizing on popular credulity.[20] This time the false Sebastian resembled his royal counterpart more closely than the gay *Rei de Penamacor,* having white skin and a red beard. Mateus Álvares[21] was the son of a mason from the Island of Terceira. After spending a few months in a monastery near Óbidos, he became a hermit and settled near Ericeira in the spring of 1585.[22] People passing by at night could hear him doing penance, administering self-flagellation and lamenting in a loud voice about his own sins and the misfortunes of Portugal.[23] The rumor soon spread that the hermit of Ericeira was Sebastian himself and, as in the case of the *Rei de Penamacor,* Mateus Álvares did nothing to correct the mistake. Álvares grew bolder as his fame increased and the number of his followers grew. One of the first to accept his identity as Sebastian was a wealthy farmer named Pero Afonso, a confirmed opponent of Spanish domination, who gathered an army of some 800 men and helped turn the hermitage into a royal residence. Álvares was proclaimed King of Portugal by his followers. Afonso was general of the army, receiving as reward for his services the name of Meneses and the titles of Marquis of Tôrres Vedras, Count of Monsanto, *Senhor* of Cascais, and *Alcaide-mor* of Lisbon. Álvares further honored Afonso by marrying his daughter and making her Queen of Portugal. Royal seals were designed and the new king issued proclamations which were sent to towns and cities in the area. He was even so bold as to send a letter to the Spanish governor, Cardinal-Archduke Alberto, telling him to leave Portugal and return to Castile.

It was time for the authorities to take some action. Álvares' army had grown to over 1,000 men and the entire countryside seemed ready to take up the revolt. There was talk of a march on Lisbon. The rebels had already captured a judge and his scribe who were investigating the disturbance and had laid siege to the estate of Gaspar Pereira, a member of the Council of State. At last the *corregedor do crime da côrte,* Diogo da Fonseca (the same one who talked to the young man in Arzila after the Battle of Alcazarquivir), was sent out at the head of Spanish troops to bring in the leaders. They were too late to save the lives of the judge, the scribe, Gaspar Pereira, and his nephew who were executed as traitors by Pero Afonso's orders; but they did meet and defeat the rebel forces in two engagements, capturing the false king and his general. The testimony of the prisoners indicated that they were motivated by a sincere desire to drive the Spaniards from Portugal. Álvares claimed that he intended to use the name of Sebastian only in encouraging the people to rebel against the Spanish authorities. Once the country had been liberated, he would have exposed his identity and called for the lawful election of a ruler. The rebels were dealt with severely. On June 14, 1585, Mateus Álvares was hanged and quartered in Lisbon, and his head was mounted on a post in public view for a month. Pero Afonso and his accomplices were also executed, twenty other men were hanged in Ericeira, and many others were sent to the galleys.

The severe treatment given to all those suspected of engaging in any activity aimed toward the overthrow of the Spanish government discouraged further demonstrations by the *sebastianistas* in Portugal until the Restoration of 1640. Portuguese exiles in Spain, France, England, and Italy, however, continued their efforts for some time.

The next false Sebastian appeared in Madrigal, Spain, in 1594. Although it appears that no effective contact had been made with sympathizers in France and Portugal by the time the principal figures were apprehended, the plot was engineered by a follower of Dom António who hoped to use the *sebastianistas* in placing the Prior of Crato on the throne of Portugal. The attempt was not successful and, in all probability, the secrecy with which the investigation was conducted prevented any information about its existence from circulating within the Portuguese borders. It is not known whether word of the plot had reached Dom António. The case of Gabriel de Espinosa, the Pastry-maker of Madrigal, as the Spanish impostor was called, will be taken up in detail in the following chapter.

The fourth and last attempt to impersonate Sebastian of Portugal is interesting, not because of the pretender himself as in the case of the *Pastelero de Madrigal,* but because of the participation of João de Castro. The appearance of this false Sebastian in Venice was complete proof to João de Castro that his interpretations of the *trovas* of Bandarra were correct, and this conviction prompted him to write about Sebastian's return with a sincerity and faith that were instrumental in keeping the embers of *sebastianismo* alive until the Restoration again revived the flame.[24]

João de Castro was the illegitimate son of the superintendent of finances during Sebastian's reign. After António was acclaimed King of Portugal, Castro joined his forces, fighting at Alcântara and later accompanying the Prior of Crato into exile in England and France. After the failure of the expedition to the Azores (in which he participated), Castro became disgusted with the poverty of Dom António's little court in England and moved to France, refusing to take part in the English-supported expedition of 1589. He became interested in the *trovas* of Bandarra and decided that the *Encoberto* must be Sebastian who was still alive. After Dom António's death in 1595, many of the expatriates made their peace with Spain and returned to Portugal, but João de Castro stayed in Paris, the center of resistance against Spanish domination. In 1597 Castro began to write about his interpretations of the old prophetic verses, announcing the return of Sebastian. His statements seemed to be confirmed the following year when he heard through a Portuguese exile in Venice that Sebastian was there.

The man in question appeared in Venice in June, 1598. Reports were contradictory, but it seemed that he had lived in Verona for a while under the name of Dom Diogo, later moving to Ferrara and then Venice. Although he refused to speak Portuguese and chose companions of doubtful reputation from the lower ranks of society, the stranger claimed to be Portuguese and a Knight of the Cross. His stories about the Battle of Alcazarquivir and about his own adventures during the twenty-year period between the battle and his arrival in Venice gradually led the Portuguese expatriates there to believe that he was really King Sebastian. The Spanish ambassador in Venice, Diego de Mendoza, had heard that the stranger was one Marco Tulio Catizone (or Carzón), a native of the department of Calabria; therefore, he urged the Venetian authorities to arrest the man and verify his true identity. Tulio was imprisoned in November, and several members of the Portuguese colony in Venice, now convinced by the interest of Mendoza that Tulio was their king, wrote to João de Castro.

The story told by the prisoner was a clever combination of the activities ascribed to Sebastian and products of the prisoner's imagination. He was indeed, he said, King Sebastian of Portugal who had escaped from the bloody Battle of Alcazarquivir. He had returned to Portugal; however, not wanting to disturb the country by his appearance and fearing the ill will of Cardinal Henrique, he decided to continue living in disguise until the time that his return would be more welcome. After wandering through Africa, Europe, and parts of Asia, he decided to end his life in penance, but the hermit who accompanied him persuaded him that it was

God's will for him to return to Portugal and reclaim his realm. He was on the way to Rome to make himself known to the Pope when he was robbed of all his possessions, including the documents which would prove his identity. He had made a vow not to speak Portuguese, hence his refusal to use that language.

Many Portuguese came to Venice to visit the prisoner. Some found that he had no resemblance to the former King of Portugal; others, almost convinced in advance by their great desire to find Sebastian alive, were sure that their king had reappeared. The group in Paris led by João de Castro was busy soliciting the official recognition of the English and French governments so that the prisoner's release might be effected, but there was not enough proof. Fray Estêvão de Sampaio went to Venice as Castro's representative; and although he was not allowed to see Tulio, he reported that the prisoner was definitely Sebastian. Fray Estêvão then traveled to Portugal to get an official description of Sebastian[25] and in 1600 returned to Venice where he was joined by João de Castro and a number of Portuguese from Paris.

Although Castro had failed to win support from foreign governments, he had succeeded in arousing the interest of many important Portuguese in exile. Even the youngest son of Dom António traveled to Venice to help obtain the prisoner's release. The Portuguese were clamoring for their king, the Spanish ambassador was pressing for punishment, and the Doge of Venice believed that the prisoner was mad. At last the Venetian authorities chose the easiest way out of an increasingly complicated situation and freed Tulio without taking a stand. He was released to his Portuguese followers on December 15, 1600, with orders to leave Venice immediately. In spite of the fact that Tulio was dark-complexioned and his command of Portuguese indicated that he had learned it during the two years in prison, the Portuguese present, led by João de Castro, fell on their knees with great joy, acknowledging him as their rightful sovereign. None of them had known Sebastian; therefore, it was easy for them to close their eyes to the truth and see only what they wanted to believe.

The liberty of the newly-found king was short-lived. The plan was to take him to safety in France, but on passing through Florence, he was again arrested. This time all efforts to obtain his release failed, and four months later the prisoner was handed over to Spanish authorities in Naples. When his identity as Marco Tulio Catizone was established beyond doubt, the prisoner finally made a full confession, maintaining, however, that the impersonation was forced upon him by the Portuguese. In view of the uproar made by the expatriate *sebastianistas,* Philip III believed it advisable to send Tulio to the galleys where he could be exhibited as an impostor rather than taking the risk of creating a martyr by executing him. In May, 1602, the *proceso* was closed and Tulio joined the Spanish fleet as a galley slave.

After Tulio fell into Spanish hands, the Portuguese *sebastianistas* who were accompanying him scattered. Many, disillusioned perhaps by their close contact with him, decided that they were mistaken in their belief that Tulio was really Sebastian. João de Castro returned to Paris, and although he stood firm in his conviction, he had no further contact with the pretender. Another small group continued to work for Tulio's release. The conditions of his imprisonment in Naples and with the Spanish fleet were relaxed enough to permit Tulio to maintain a lively correspondence with his agents. The most indefatigable in their efforts to obtain support for the pretender were Fray Estêvão de Sampaio and Fray Boaventura de Santo António who traveled through Spain and Portugal, getting in touch with *sebastianistas,* carrying messages, and trying to arrange Tulio's escape. In March, 1603, one of the messages was intercepted by Spanish authorities. The conspiracy had grown alarmingly and the Spanish government was once more compelled to deal harshly with the *sebastianistas.* A *proceso* was begun in San Lúcar against Tulio and his accomplices, and arrests were made on a large scale. Most of the prisoners talked freely. They were operating in good faith, believing that they were supporting their lawful ruler. Only when they were shown a picture of the real Sebastian did Fray Estêvão and Fray Boaventura recognize their tragic error. Marco

Tulio reconfirmed under torture the statements he had made to the Spanish authorities in Naples. On September 23, 1603, Tulio and three accomplices were executed for treason in the main square of San Lúcar. They were hanged and quartered, with heads and right hands then exhibited in a public place. A month later, Fray Estêvão and Fray Boaventura were degraded and handed over to civil authority for equal castigation. Many others were given lighter sentences.

It was a high price to pay for their faith and loyalty to a false ideal, and one can imagine that the disillusionment suffered by the Portuguese accomplices was even more bitter for them than the ignoble death on the gallows. Their sincerity is to be admired, yet small sympathy can be aroused by such blind determination to believe in an impostor whose pose was so transparent to others. João de Castro, at least, was spared the final humiliation of being forced to accept reality, believing until his death that Sebastian I of Portugal had returned and was martyred by the Spaniards. Castro spent the rest of his life in obscurity and poverty in Paris, dedicated to his writings about the return of Sebastian. Only his *Discurso da vida do . . . Rei Dom Sebastião* and the . . . *Paráfrase do Bandarra . . . ,* written before Tulio's execution, were published, but these works constitute the evangel of the *sebastianistas*.[26]

With the death of Marco Tulio, the messianic fervor which had been building up among the *sebastianistas* was momentarily stifled. The life span of the real Sebastian, had he lived to old age, passed. Later *sebastianistas* lost all contact with reality, looking for a reincarnation of Sebastian in later Portuguese monarchs or the appearance of a phantom-like, ageless Sebastian who would return from the hidden isle, the *ilha encoberta*.[27] The *trovas* of Bandarra continued to be the principal source of inspiration. In each national crisis new apocryphal *trovas* were mixed with the old, inciting the people to resist whatever danger threatened the nation. There was a new surge of interest in the *trovas* in 1640 when it was believed that João IV would fulfil the prophecies.[28] Then, when João IV failed to be the long-sought messiah, interest shifted back to Sebastian, then to Alfonso VI, then to Dom Pedro, and even to the latter's infant son, João, who lived only a few days after birth. The prime interpreter of the *trovas* during the second half of the seventeenth century was Father António Vieira, a brilliant orator and highly erudite man, who suffered two years in prison and many years of attack from the Inquisition largely because of his interest in the prophecies. But, in spite of the Inquisition's efforts, *sebastianismo* still flourished. A foreigner traveling in Portugal in the early eighteenth century reported that half of the Portuguese were waiting for the messiah and the other half for Sebastian.[29] A century later the French invasion created another wave of *sebastianista* fervor, and the strength of the movement was clearly indicated by the violence of the attacks made upon it by its opponents.[30]

This was the last serious interest in the prophecies although incidents of messianic fervor continued in Brazil through the nineteenth century. The most well-known is the revolt led by Antônio Conselheiro at Canudos in 1896. In Portugal rural areas still contain those who believe that Sebastian will return; but, on the whole, the general attitude now is that *sebasianismo* is a ridiculous cult followed only by crackpots and simpletons.

IV

GABRIEL
DE
ESPINOSA

*O*n the night of October 7, 1594, Don Rodrigo de Santillán was making the customary rounds in fulfilment of his duties as *alcalde de corte y del crimen* of the *chancillería* of Valladolid when reports of a badly dressed man possessing valuable jewels aroused his interest.[1] The original denunciation came from a woman who had been allowed to drink from the stranger's cup, carved from the horn of a unicorn. Thinking that such a costly possession could have reached his hands only through theft, the woman reported the incident. Even more curious were other tales of the man's words and actions. When asked whose likeness appeared on the ring he wore, he replied, "It is your lord." On closer examination the portrait was identified as His Royal Highness King Philip II of Spain. When those present jokingly asked the stranger if it was not his lord, as well, his answer was, "No, not mine. Some day I will be his lord and yours." His companions attempted to make him explain this strange statement, but he gave evasive answers and changed the topic of conversation. A few days before, while walking near the edge of the city, the stranger was said to have come upon some men exhibiting their horsemanship. He mounted one of the horses and gave a demonstration of skill and daring that both awed and delighted the spectators. The reports seemed contradictory: the stranger was poorly dressed and moved in social circles which were anything but aristocratic, yet he exhibited valuable jewels and assumed airs far above his apparent station.

The suspicion that the man was a thief and the desire to dispel the aura of mystery surrounding him prompted Don Rodrigo to search until, later that night, he found the stranger in a humble rooming house. When Don Rodrigo and his men first entered the man's room, they found him trying to break open the window casement to escape. Although he blamed his agitation on the late hour, the unceremonious entrance of the law party, and the fact that his nerves were on edge because his servants had recently robbed him of 200 ducats, the stranger's attempted flight bespoke a guilty conscience. He identified himself as Gabriel de Espinosa from Madrigal, cook and pastry-maker in the service of Doña Ana de Austria. He was dressed in underclothes of fine linen, and his toilette met standards much higher than those of an ordinary cook. In the room Don Rodrigo found a watch, some silver statues, and the ring with the king's likeness, all of which, according to Espinosa, had been entrusted to him by Doña Ana. After further questioning about the unicorn cup, Espinosa led the *alcalde* to another modest inn where he had left with the innkeeper the cup, a silver goblet, some fine underclothing, and a lock of woman's hair.

Suspecting that Espinosa had really stolen the expensive items, Don Rodrigo took him to jail pending verification of his story by Doña Ana; however, Espinosa's deportment soon convinced the *alcalde* that he was no common thief. There was something very strange about the man, and Don Rodrigo was sure that he could have gotten at the truth immediately if only the law had permitted him to put the prisoner to torture. Legal procedure demanded a formal accusation of crime before torture could be used in questioning, and Espinosa was not to be intimidated by threats. On the contrary, he reprimanded the *alcalde's* severe attitude, reminding him haughtily that the king had not put him in office to maltreat strangers without cause.

As soon as he had placed Espinosa in a cell alone and had arranged to have all messages and mail intercepted, Don Rodrigo sent a letter to Madrigal de las Altas Torres, a small town some seventy-five kilometers south of Valladolid, notifying Doña Ana of Espinosa's arrest and asking for confirmation of the pastry-maker's statement. Don Rodrigo was particularly desirous of handling this matter with efficiency and speed; Doña Ana de Austria, a nun in the Augustinian convent of Nuestra Señora de Gracia la Real, was of royal blood, and some of the items found in Espinosa's possession were crown jewels.

Doña Ana, who was to celebrate her twenty-sixth birthday that very month, was born out of wedlock to Doña María de Mendoza and Don Juan de Austria, illegitimate son of the Emperor Charles V and half-brother of Philip II. Don Juan took the baby a few days after birth and entrusted her to Doña Magdalena de Ulloa, his own foster mother. When the child was six years old, she was placed in the convent at Madrigal. After Don Juan's death in 1578, Doña Ana's existence was made known to the king who recognized her as his niece, giving her the name of Austria and the right to the title of *excelencia*. In compliance with the king's wishes, she continued to stay in the convent at Madrigal where she was given special privileges and was permitted to have personal servants.

Don Rodrigo de Santillán's precautions were well-advised. On October 8 he intercepted a messenger who came from Madrigal bearing four letters for Espinosa—two from Doña Ana and two from Fray Miguel dos Santos, prior to the Madrigal convent (which housed both nuns and friars) and *vicario* (friar in immediate charge of the female congregation) of the nuns. From the contents of these letters, Don Rodrigo realized that he had stumbled upon some mysterious activity of great importance. The man whom he arrested was no simple cook for both Doña Ana and Fray Miguel addressed him as "señor" and Fray Miguel called him "Your Majesty." There were strange references to a company of followers, to Espinosa's return to Madrigal in disguise, and to a child who evidently belonged to Doña Ana and Espinosa. Doña Ana's letters were couched in extremely affectionate language, and she intimated that Espinosa had promised to marry her.[2] Although the letters did not reveal

Espinosa's true identity or the nature of the venture undertaken by the correspondents, the situation smacked of treason. Accordingly, Don Rodrigo wrote a full report to Philip II on October 9, sending the intercepted letters and asking for a royal commission with full power to investigate and prosecute.

In sixteenth-century Spain the judicial hierarchy was composed of two grades: the *corregidor* or *alcalde* who handled civil and criminal cases (often with power to accuse, prosecute, imprison, and judge), and the courts of appeal. The highest court of appeal was the Council of Castile which also functioned as a supreme administrative council, particularly in juridical matters. As *alcalde de [casa y] corte,* Don Rodrigo was one of the robed judges who sat in the *sala de alcaldes* of the Council of Castile; and as *alcalde del crimen,* he sat in the *sala del crimen* of the Valladolid *chancillería* as well as having jurisdiction over his own territory. The *chancillería* of Valladolid was one of the two oldest and most important regional courts in Spain.[3] Thus, Don Rodrigo was well qualified to pursue the investigation.

On October 12 he sent a second letter to the king repeating the request for immediate action (*leg.* 172, f. 4). He now suspected that Espinosa was really Dom António, Prior of Crato, pretender to the throne of Portugal. The confessor of the nuns at the convent, brought there at Doña Ana's request, was Portuguese as were the servants in Espinosa's pastry shop. As well, several Portuguese had appeared at the jail, asking about Espinosa. Although Espinosa insisted that he was a humble pastry-maker, Don Rodrigo believed that his manners indicated a higher social station. In physical characteristics Espinosa could meet the description of Dom António in that he was small of stature, blue-eyed, and could be sixty-four years old although his blond hair was not completely white. One eye contained a cloud, or pterygium. Furthermore, Don Rodrigo reasoned, Dom António was the only person qualified to receive the title of majesty whose absence from his own country would not be immediately noted.

Of all the reasons given by Don Rodrigo for his identification, perhaps the most convincing was the participation of Fray Miguel dos Santos. Fray Miguel was preacher to the royal house of Portugal prior to 1580[4] and had taken an open stand with the Portuguese nationalist faction in favor of recognizing Dom António's claim to the throne of Portugal. He had served as courier to Rome for Dom António, who was trying to establish his legitimacy, collaborated in the acclamation of Dom António as king in the Senate of Lisbon, and fought with the Prior of Crato's forces at Alcântara.[5] After the annexation of Portugal to Spain, Fray Miguel was transferred to Castile where he could be watched more closely and his political activities curtailed.[6] Around 1589 he was appointed *vicario* of the Madrigal convent at the request of Doña Ana, who had met and liked him.[7] He was a clever and intelligent man, twice provincial of his order, highly respected among the Portuguese as a man of letters.[8] It is no wonder that he soon began to exert great influence over Doña Ana de Austria.

The royal commission and instructions for proceeding with the investigation reached Valladolid on October 14. Don Rodrigo left for Madrigal at two o'clock the following morning, having entrusted Espinosa, still in jail, to the care of his brother, Don Diego de Santillán. Upon reaching Madrigal late in the afternoon, the *alcalde* went immediately to the monastery in the hope of arresting Doña Ana and Fray Miguel before they could hear of his presence and destroy any papers which might incriminate them. He was too late. Espinosa had succeeded in communicating with them after his arrest, and their writing desks were empty of recent correspondence. Don Rodrigo confined Doña Ana to her cell, posting four nuns as guards, then arrested Fray Miguel and all other persons whose names had appeared in the intercepted letters: a Portuguese doctor named Manuel Mendes, the Portuguese confessor, a trusted servant of Doña Ana named Blas Nieto, the child who lived with Espinosa, and the child's nursemaid (*leg.* 172, f. 110).

Early in the morning of October 17, Don Rodrigo began the interrogation of Fray Miguel dos Santos whom he believed to be the key witness. Doña Ana might be easy prey to any deceit perpetrated by Espinosa since she had entered the convent at a very early age and lacked worldly experience, but Fray Miguel would be difficult to hoodwink. He was a man of intelligence, experience, and sound judgment; and he would not address Espinosa in terms of great respect without good reason. Because of the suspected nature of the crime and the implication of Doña Ana, Don Rodrigo made every effort to preserve the greatest secrecy, rejecting the services of a scribe and writing Fray Miguel's statement with his own hand (*leg.* 172, fols. 7 and 112). At first Fray Miguel refused to answer; but after the *alcalde* had convinced him that the seriousness of the crime permitted the use of torture even against ecclesiastical prisoners, Fray Miguel admitted that he had written the two letters to Espinosa. Espinosa only pretended to be a humble cook, Fray Miguel said. In reality, he was King Sebastian of Portugal who had made a vow of penance after the Battle of Alcazarquivir. Don Rodrigo did not consider the story at all convincing, believing still that Fray Miguel was trying to hide the fact that Espinosa was really Dom António (upon whose head a price had been placed by Philip II); but further questioning was prevented by the sudden appearance of the Augustinian provincial superior and by a jurisdictional dispute between civil and ecclesiastical powers, eventually resolved by the appointment of an ecclesiastical judge to assist with the investigation.

Fray Gabriel de Goldaraz, provincial superior of the Order of Saint Augustine, was enraged by the *alcalde's* actions. Santillán had entered the cloister without permission, had seized ecclesiastical prisoners, and was conducting his investigations in a high-handed manner that endangered the honor of Doña Ana de Austria and of the monastery; consequently, the provincial ordered his flock not to answer the *alcalde's* questions under penalty of excommunication.

Although Don Rodrigo was an officer of the civil court and normally would not have jurisdiction over ecclesiastics, in this case he felt justified in entering the monastery and arresting whomever he deemed necessary. He suspected that the crime involved was that of lese majesty, in which case the king's ministers possessed full powers to proceed against ecclesiastical prisoners. Don Rodrigo's letters, protesting the provincial's interference, provide a graphic example of the bitter feeling between civil and ecclesiastical officials. The most vehement was written on October 20 to Don Martín de Idiáquez, Philip's secretary:

por la carta de su mg^t entendera v. m. el estado en que estan estos negocios. yo prometo a v. m. como quien soy que si los frayles me uvieran dexado y no estorvadome tan impertinentemente que yo tuviera [este] negocio ya fuera de duda y que el vicario uviera dicho todo lo que ay. pero como sintio alas y fabor en su provincial rretirose luego. y yo estoy aguardando a que su mg^t a de hazer una muy grande demostracion sobre eso. y prometo a v. m. que si no se haze no se como hemos de poder hazer justicia pues los frayles ya no sirven en el mundo sin de impedirla y enmarañar y encubrir los negocios. y de rreligiosos rrecogidos se an hecho cavilosos y tramperos solicitadores y el patio de chancilleria esta casi tan lleno de frayles como de legos. den orden vs. mds. por amor de dios de que se quieten y rrecojan que a mi parecer es una materia importantisima de estado pues nunca ha avido ni en Portugal ni en Castilla levantamientos ni alborotos en que no tengan mucha parte los frayles y cierto que si no pareciese poca devocion diria que como en otro tiempo se hazian soldados por bivir con libertad se hazen agora frayles. y a mi me tienen agora tan enojado que v. m. me la a de hazer en perdonarme el averme alargado.* (*leg.* 172, f. 16).

In the meantime, Fray Gabriel was conducting his own investigation, the results of which he reported to Philip II. Doña Ana testified that she had first met Espinosa through her friend and servant, Doña Luisa de Grado, to whom he had related his adventures in the Holy Land. He also said that he had been a soldier with her father, Don Juan de Austria, and that he had been captured by Dom António's forces in Portugal and carried into France. She considered Espinosa to be a gentleman in disguise: "hombre honrado y hidalgo...que era persona de mas estima que su officio decia y que esto daba a entender en sus palabras...y en particular decia que andaba disimulado en aquel officio por una desgracia que le avia sucedido" (*leg.* 172, f. 94).* Most of the nuns and friars believed the child who came to Madrigal with Espinosa to be Doña Ana's

*Translations of starred passages may be found in Appendix B.

niece, and Doña Ana also considered that to be the case although Espinosa had already hinted that the little girl had some relationship to her. For some time Doña Ana had believed that she had a brother named Francisco, and she rather suspected the child might be his.

This opinion arose from an event which had taken place some nine years before. A young pilgrim came to the convent asking for Doña Ana; but for some unexplained reason Doña Ana refused to speak to her, sending the prioress and Doña Luisa to the cloister grating in her place. The pilgrim told them that she was Doña Ana's sister and that they had a brother who was born with a birthmark on his shoulder but who had been lost. Doña Luisa was sure that the pilgrim was a man in disguise because she saw that the young stranger was wearing men's clothes under the pilgrim's garb and walked like a man. Doña Ana further stated that Espinosa had offered to make contact with this lost brother and to bring him to Madrigal by All Saints or Christmas. He had gone to Valladolid for that purpose, and she had given him the jewels to take care of the expenses of the trip.

In general, the testimony of the other nuns supported Doña Ana's story, but when it came to the matter of Espinosa's identity, opinions were quite diverse. One friar testified that he had known Espinosa previously in Pamplona and he considered Espinosa "hechizero farsante y hablador" (a loudmouthed, lying sorcerer) (*leg.* 172, f. 94). This same opinion was reported by a nun who had talked to a man from Salamanca who knew Espinosa there, and to a stranger who had known him in Portugal during the war. Others had heard that he had a pact with the devil and was dangerous. Many testified that they had heard he was a noble in disguise. All agreed that Espinosa and Fray Miguel were on very friendly terms. A few ventured the opinion, on the basis of Fray Miguel's esteem, that Espinosa might be Dom António; but the majority rejected that possibility because of Doña Ana's open hostility toward the Prior of Crato, whom she considered a traitor.

This, in brief, was the information gathered by Provincial Goldaraz and sent to Madrid on October 21 in the hope of convincing the king that Don Rodrigo was making a great commotion over something which was really not too serious. Goldaraz' reputation as an official of the Hermits of Saint Augustine was at stake, and he was eager to avoid any trouble that would reflect on the proper administration of his province. Although he did not tell Philip II, Goldaraz had forseen the difficulties which might arise from Fray Miguel's friendship with Espinosa and had written Fray Miguel on September 17, warning him to be careful (*leg.* 172, f. 251). While believing that Doña Ana had been thoughtless and irresponsible, Goldaraz placed the real blame for the trouble on Fray Miguel whose express duty it was to care for her.[9] The provincial's efforts to minimize the scandal were thwarted: in spite of the protests of Goldaraz and the papal nucio, the crime was designated officially as treason; Goldaraz was ordered out of the monastery; and an ecclesiastical judge, Doctor Juan de Llano Valdés, was appointed on November 2 to take over the interrogation of ecclesiastical prisoners (*leg.* 172, f. 26).[10]

Concurrently with the jurisdictional dispute with Provincial Goldaraz, Don Rodrigo was involved in another quarrel about delineation of authority, this time with his immediate superior, the president of the *chancillería of* Valladolid. Junco de Posada, irritated because Don Rodrigo had acted without first consulting him and, perhaps, because he felt that he himself should be in charge of the investigation, wrote to Philip II on October 15 complaining that Don Rodrigo was not conducting the investigation with as much secrecy as the nature of the matter demanded (*leg.* 172, f. 105). He assigned two of his own men to help Don Diego de Santillán guard Espinosa, and the next day he wrote the king again, this time requesting permission to assign *Alcalde* Portocarrero to the case as coadjutor to Don Rodrigo (*leg.* 172, f. 107).

This was a direct offense to Don Rodrigo's honor and his complaints were strong and frequent. Of the five letters he wrote to Madrid protesting against the president's action, the one addressed to Cristóbal de Mora, dated October 18, contains the frankest expression of his fears:

Yo señor en el discurso de mi vida avra V. Sᵃ entendido y echado de
ver quan poco cudicioso soy y quanto mas estimo la honrra que la
hazienda y esto procuro rrondando de noche y trabajando de dia como
todo el mundo sabe. y pues segun muestran los principios de este negocio parece que se me podria esto seguir con algunas ventajas suplico a V.
Sᵃ no permita que me la vengan a quitar agora los que mientras yo estoy
rrondando y trabajando se estan durmiendo y puteando. y no permita V.
Sᵃ que se me haga esta afrenta. y no es justo que den coadjutor que goze
de el fruto de mis trabajos. y para solo suplicar esto a V. Sᵃ despacho este
correo fiado en la merced que V. Sᵃ me haze y en la rrazon que tengo.
y prometo cierto que me tiene esto el mas mohino que he estado en mi
vida.* (*leg.* 172, f. 120)

Although Don Rodrigo was sure that Junco de Posada and his
good friend, Martín Hernández Portocarrero, were conspiring to
ruin his reputation and steal the profitable assignment from him,
Portocarrero, at least, was not at all eager to participate in the
Madrigal investigation. He had been called off another case for
the Madrigal assignment, and since Don Rodrigo's choler was running so high, his position at best was an uncomfortable one. After
reporting to Madrigal, Portocarrero wrote twice to His Majesty
stating that his presence there was not required and asking permission to return to Valladolid. He stayed in Madrigal until the arrival
of the ecclesiastical judge on November 15, then he returned to
Valladolid, leaving Don Rodrigo in sole charge of the lay prisoners
and Juan de Llano in charge of the religious investigation.

Junco de Posada's most frequent complaint to the king about Don
Rodrigo—that he was not providing ample guards for Espinosa and,
thus, was not preserving the secrecy necessary to the investigation—
seems to have been without foundation. On October 19 Don Rodrigo
had Espinosa moved from Valladolid to the Castillo de la Mota in
Medina del Campo, a secure prison which was closer to Madrigal.
Although Posada was in Valladolid and could know nothing about
conditions in the Medina prison, he wrote Philip II on three occasions to relay reports that Espinosa was not well-guarded and that
his meals were being served on silver plates in the house of Simón
Ruiz, where Don Rodrigo stayed when he visited Medina. Santillán,

of course, was powerless to stop gossip, undoubtedly augmented by the numerous arrests and jurisdictional disputes, and a speedy termination of the case was impeded by the necessity of reporting every detail directly to Philip II and awaiting his instructions. The accusation that Espinosa was treated so royally, however, is belied by a letter to Don Rodrigo from Simón Ruiz on December 3. Espinosa had fallen ill with the *tercianas* and, according to his guards, was suffering from acute melancholy because of the severe treatment he had been given by Don Rodrigo. His confinement was so strict that no one was permitted to enter his cell; but since the guards had led Ruiz to believe that Espinosa was on the point of death, Ruiz requested permission to allow a doctor or a priest to attend him. Ruiz claimed only to be moved by the prisoner's pitiful condition and begged Don Rodrigo, "conbiene no le dexar asi morir desesperado" (*leg.* 172, f. 226).* Espinosa's fever was not fatal; five days later he was strong enough to be questioned by the apostolic judge, Juan de Llano.

Espinosa's success in mystifying those around him was subject to great variation. Don Rodrigo, having discarded his first theory that Espinosa might be Dom António, was now convinced that the *pastelero* was a common rogue although he admitted that Espinosa's appearance abetted his impersonation of an important personage. In early November Santillán had forced Espinosa to admit that Fray Miguel and Doña Ana believed him to be Sebastian, but Espinosa said that he had not tried to dissuade them because they were kind to him and gave him presents (*leg.* 172, f. 28). After talking to Espinosa, *Alcalde* Portocarrero reported that he was a "pastelero embustero" (lying pastry cook) who should be punished swiftly and severely before the error into which Fray Miguel had fallen gained general credence and caused real trouble (*leg.* 172, f. 175). Don Diego de Santillán, however, was convinced that the prisoner was "hombre prinsipal [*sic*] aunque el procure harto hazerse pastelero" (*leg.* 172, f. 19).* Don Diego escorted Espinosa from Valladolid to Medina del Campo and was greatly impressed by the prisoner's ability to speak French and German. When he was asked if he spoke Portuguese, as well, Espinosa replied that although he had been in Portugal, he did not know the language. The question obviously upset him, and he spent the remainder of the trip in moody silence.

Before seeing Espinosa, Juan de Llano seemed willing to believe that the story told by Doña Ana and Fray Miguel—that Espinosa was really Sebastian of Portugal—had some factual basis despite Don Rodrigo's arguments to the contrary. Prior to the arrival of the ecclesiastical judge, Don Rodrigo had allowed Fray Miguel to persist in his error without contradiction in the hope of obtaining information about accomplices, but he later expressed the opinion that Llano's attitude was aiding the dissemination of the deceit. On December 5 Santillán wrote to Don Juan de Idiáquez, one of Philip's advisers: "yo querria mucho que luego se le mande [al doctor Llano] que atage estas publicidades que doña Ana haze de que este Espinosa es el rrey don Sebastian, porque el publicarse y el authorizarse con un semblante de un jues puede traer grandisimos inconvenientes" (*leg.* 172, f. 227).* On December 8 Llano accompanied Santillán to Medina del Campo to interview Espinosa, and the personal contact dispelled all doubts that the ecclesiastical judge may have had about the possibility of the prisoner's royal birth. Llano had seen pictures of Sebastian, and he reported that Espinosa bore no resemblance to the dead king:

...en lo que toca a su persona no me parece que se puede por ningun caso hablar en que sea el que dizen. Antes del todo es contrario a su aspecto y aparencia porque este preso es hombre muy pequeño de cuerpo y muy flaco de rostro y pocas carnes y de muy diferente color de rostro, cavello y barba. demas que tiene una grande y notable nube en el ojo derecho, en la hedad muy desigual.—es muy ladino en la lengua castellana con mucho estremo sin tener acento ni pronunciacion de otra ninguna, que pocas vezes acontece en los naturales de otros reynos. y ansi por estas razones, como por averme confesado una y muchas vezes en el discurso de la platica que con el tube, que no era el que dezian y que esto era verdad....* (*leg.* 172, f. 81)

Both Juan de Llano and Don Rodrigo were convinced early in the investigation that Doña Ana had been an innocent victim of the deceit engineered by Fray Miguel and/or Espinosa, and both judges showed their desire to treat her with gentleness and respect. At first Don Rodrigo showed some severity in his dealings with her, offended by her lack of cooperation. When he confronted her with the unsigned letters to Espinosa which he had intercepted in Valladolid, she snatched them from him and tried to tear them up. He managed to save them from destruction, but she refused to admit that she had written them. After she began to realize how dangerous her position was, Doña Ana proved to be a very willing witness, and Don Rodrigo began to relax his stern attitude. Indeed, her position was a pitiable one. Having entered the convent at a very early age, she was without experience in worldly affairs and was completely at the mercy of her spiritual adviser whom she respected and trusted. Now she was told that Fray Miguel was a liar and a traitor; and the only person to whom she could turn, her uncle Philip, believed that she was a willing partner to treachery. It was fortunate for her that the two judges were not equally disposed to consider her guilty.

Before the arrival of Juan de Llano, Doña Ana refused to make any declaration on the grounds that, as a member of the royal family, she would answer only to the king. By November 13 she had heard that an ecclesiastical judge was arriving soon and knowing that she would be forced to answer his questions, she asked Santillán to obtain permission for her to write directly to the king in a last desperate effort to avoid the status of an ordinary prisoner. She would testify before a judge, she said, only if Philip II specifically commanded her to do so or if he withheld permission for her to communicate directly with him. If she was forced to testify, she preferred that the judge be Don Rodrigo whom she knew to be a gentleman and a just officer of the law (*leg.* 172, fols. 40 and 90). On November 18 Philip gave Doña Ana permission to write to him: that is, the king notified Don Rodrigo and Doctor Llano, who had reached Madrigal on November 15, that permission was granted and that they should use this correspondence in cross-examining her (*leg.* 172, fols. 41 and 190). Not once did Philip write directly to Doña Ana; her only contact with her uncle was through the two investigating officers.

The two letters written by Doña Ana to Philip II—one dated November 19, given to Doctor Llano and the other dated November 23, sent by Don Rodrigo—contain practically the same information. In general, they present a protest against the offense to her honor and a plea for mercy and understanding. As the king's niece, she thought she should be exempt from explaining her actions to officers of the law like any common criminal. Philip alone—as uncle, guardian, and sovereign—ought to hear her defense and pass judgment on her actions; and surely, he should know that she was incapable of any act that might be offensive to him. She had accepted Espinosa as Sebastian in good faith:

... aviendo yo tenido relacion con evidencia de que el Rey don Sebastian mi primo no era muerto, y teniendo alguna luz de que andava por el mundo peregrinando, hize movida de lastima algunas devociones para que Dios descubriesse si era verdad o mentira. y en este intermedio vino a este lugar este hombre que se llamava Gabriel de Espinosa el qual se descubrio a fray Miguel de los Santos y a mi ser el mismo Rey don Sebastian. y lo testifico con evidentes razones y señales muchas y muy particulares por las quales me persuadio creello, aunque es verdad que otras razones que oia de su oficio me despintavan esta verdad.* (*leg.* 172, f. 211)

y preguntandole yo que porque andava assi me dixo que lo avia jurado sobre el santo sepulchro, y entendidas sus razones que queria el ganarle primero que descubrirse, hablavame siempre con tanta afficion del servicio de V. M^d y tan sin codicia de quitar un palmo de tierra de su corona que este fue el anzuelo principal con que me engaño, juntamente con ver yo que era sobrino de V. M^d tan querido, y que el dia que el paresciera diziendo verdad, V. M^d se holgara dello.* (*leg.* 172, f. 191)

She had not informed Philip of this earlier because at first she was not convinced that it was true; and later, when she had completely accepted Espinosa as Sebastian, he made her promise not to reveal his identity until his vow was terminated. Doña Ana firmly denied the existence of any treacherous plot. Espinosa had gone to Valladolid to get her brother and the references to their returning to

Madrigal in disguise did not indicate plans for her escape from the convent: "esta era la venida y los cavallos a solo verme, y no sacarme del monasterio como han dicho, que quien por no disgustar a V. M^d se encerro en el sin voluntad, no saliera del sin la de V. M^d pues en este estado y los trabajos y padecimientos del, solo tengo por alivio que servi a V. M^d y lo tengo por bastante pago" (*leg.* 172, f. 191).* Again and again she reminded Philip II that she was his niece and that her honor, which was in part his own, was at stake. If she erred, it was through ignorance: "... supplico a V. M^d por Jesu Cristo crucificado se compadezca de mi y mire que esta honrra que tanto sus ministros de V. M^d despedaçan es de una sobrina hija de aquel desdichado padre y que mi yerro fue simpleza y el castigo mucho para el. si esse hombre es malo o bueno ayanlo con el y no permita V. M^d que lo pague esta desdichada y esta casa y tantos presos inocentes que no tienen culpa" (*leg.* 172, f. 191).*

At the same time that she wrote to the king, Doña Ana gave the judges two letters for Espinosa in which she begged him to reveal his identity. Needless to say, the letters were sent to the king and not to the prisoner, but their obvious sincerity was influential in convincing Juan de Llano and Don Rodrigo of Doña Ana's innocence:

y assi os supplico por quanto puedo os declareis con don Rodrigo de Santillan diziendole quien sois, pues su M^d y sus ministros tendran mucho contento de que vos seais mi primo el Rey don Sebastian. y fio de la gran Christiandad de Su M^d que sin resp° humano os recibira con el amor que si fueredeis hijo suyo pues vos nunca tratasteis de ofendelle ni aveis hecho cosa por donde Su M^d dexe de hazer lo que es justo. Vos señor lo deveis a mi honrra que es caso piadoso lo que della se dize por solo averos yo desseado servir y querido y estimado como a mi primo. y siendolo vos esto bastara para que acudais por ella, que solo pende de declarar quien sois....* (*leg.* 172, f. 211)

From the king's correspondence with Llano and Santillán, it is clear that Philip never considered the possibility that Espinosa might really be his nephew Sebastian. The prospect seemed so absurd that Philip refused to make any direct reference to Sebastian, and his instructions to the two investigators indicated that the emphasis should be on finding out who Espinosa really was: "en suma se guie de manera que averiguando quien es por sus baxos passos y quilates queden convencidas sus mentiras passadas y deshecho el enrredo y engaño sin encaminarlo de suerte que añadiese de lugar que pueda dezir que tiene aquellos devaneos y falsidades por verdad" (*leg.* 172, f. 206).*

Throughout the year-long investigation, the item that caused Philip II the most concern was the two-year-old child whom Espinosa had brought to Madrigal and whom the nuns and friars considered to be Doña Ana's niece. Doña Ana also believed that the little girl might be her brother's child; consequently, she had her brought to the convent for frequent visits, showering her with gifts and affection. In the intercepted letters from Doña Ana and Fray Miguel to Espinosa, there were frequent references to the little girl. Doña Ana spoke of her as "mi hija" (my child) and said that the child called her "madre" (mother), and Fray Miguel wrote of Doña Ana and the child in phrases such as these: "Como V. Mg^d se fue, su madre la mando trayer a su casa quasi cada dia y la tiene todo el dia. y la regala al fin como tal madre a tal hija" (*leg.* 172, f. 100).* The affectionate language used by Doña Ana in her letters to Espinosa and a reference to some "alta promesa" (important promise) at first led Don Rodrigo to believe that Espinosa had promised to marry Doña Ana and that the child was theirs. This opinion was strengthened by Doña Ana's frequent statements that she did not consider herself a nun because she had professed against her will. Santillán later changed his mind, maintaining that Doña Ana was not the child's mother. Juan de Llano also believed that she was not, and their opinion was confirmed by the testimony of Doña Ana's closest friends in the convent. Philip II, however, was not as readily convinced of Doña Ana's innocence in this matter. The fact that the child was named Clara Eugenia—the name of Philip's daughter whom Sebastian had wanted to marry—disturbed the king: "...este nombre es uno de los grandes indicios que ay para mi de ser su hija que el preso no tenia para que poner este nombre ni aun el le debria saber y sobre esto se le podrian hazer preguntas" (*leg.* 172, f. 242).* In each letter of instruction to the two judges, Philip told them to find out who was the mother of the child and reminded them that "lo de la niña" (the matter of the child) was the most important item. He had placed Doña Ana and her half-sister, Doña Juana,[11] in convents expressly for the purpose of avoiding propagation of the bastard branch and he wanted to be completely certain that little Clara Eugenia was not of royal descent. Although the convent personnel testified that Espinosa had not been in Madrigal before June of that same year, Philip repeatedly requested further verification of that point; and he even had Don Rodrigo measure the small communion window in the choir to see if it was big enough for a body to pass through (*leg.* 173, f. 275). Only after he had completely satisfied himself that Inés Cid, the child's nursemaid, was her mother did Philip allow the case to be closed and the culprits punished. His advisers were ready to terminate the case in early February, but the king's doubts delayed the matter until late July.

As long as Philip II withheld permission to apply torture in the questioning of Fray Miguel and Espinosa, the equivocal position of Espinosa could not be resolved. He had never claimed to be anyone but Gabriel de Espinosa, a humble pastry-maker who came from nowhere; however, the grand manners he assumed upon occasion, the mysterious half-answers, and his contradictory statements only gave the impression that he was trying to hide the fact that he was not the person he claimed to be. On November 4, Espinosa first admitted to Santillán that Doña Ana and Fray Miguel considered him to be King Sebastian and that he had not tried to dissuade them since they treated him so well (*leg.* 172, f. 28). Later, when pressed by Don Rodrigo and Juan de Llano for more explicit information, he hinted that Fray Miguel had persuaded him to assume the identity of Sebastian for Doña Ana's benefit, but he still refused to tell any more about his own identity (*leg.* 172, fols. 50 and 81).

Nor did it prove easy to learn anything about him through others. The inhabitants of Madrigal had not known him before his arrival in June of that same year, and their scanty information was based on hearsay and gossip. Santillán had sought information in other cities—Burgos, la Coruña, Zamora, León—without success, and he was unable to question the only persons who had come to Madrigal with Espinosa: Clara Eugenia and Inés Cid. The child was only two years old, and her nursemaid was five-months pregnant, in no physical condition to be questioned under torture, which was the only method considered effective.

One of the few reliable items of information concerning Espinosa came from a man who had known him for six years only so that even his testimony did little to clarify the situation. Gregorio González, a cook in the service of the Marquis of Almazán, had met Espinosa in Madrid at Christmastime of 1588 when Espinosa was hired to help him prepare a banquet. Espinosa, who said that he was a cook in Ocaña and showed González his license, was poorly dressed and had with him a sixteen-year-old son. After that evening, González did not see Espinosa again until September of 1594 when he came to Valladolid in the retinue of the Count of Neiva. He saw Espinosa on the street one day, recognized him, and spoke to him. Espinosa came to González' rooms several times after that, displaying valuable jewels and implying that he was an important person in disguise. Among the items González saw in Espinosa's possession were a ring with the likeness of Philip II and a picture of a nun. In praising the nun's beauty, Espinosa hinted that she might marry in spite of her vows. González asked him to explain, but Espinosa answered with the adage, "para con reyes no hay leyes" (for kings there are no laws), and refused further clarification. He also offered González a job with a handsome salary, but González and his friends only laughed, considering Espinosa's words idle boasting. A few days later, González heard that Espinosa had been arrested by Don Rodrigo (*leg.* 172, f. 195). Although González thought Espinosa "loco y embustero" (crazy and a liar) and believed that he had stolen the jewels, both Santillán and Llano were sure that Espinosa was not interested primarily in financial gain. Doña Ana had offered him more jewels which he refused, and he even threatened to return those he had accepted (*leg.* 172, fols. 44 and 78). Santillán heard, as well, that Espinosa gave alms with much more generosity than his station demanded (*leg.* 172, f. 21).

Further questioning of Doña Ana added very little to the information she had already written to Philip II on November 19 and 23, serving only to confirm the two judges' opinion that she was the innocent victim of a willful deceit practised by Fray Miguel and Espinosa. Llano, in particular, was impressed by her cooperation and honesty: "a que ayuda mucho a creerlo ansi la buena relacion que entre todas gentes ansi del monasterio como de fuera del e hallado de la virtud y recogimiento de la dicha doña Ana...pues si en ella [ay alguna] malicia no parece considerable" (*leg.* 172, f. 78).* In the two confessions made before Llano on December 7 and January 26 (*leg.* 172, f. 242, and *leg.* 173, f. 234), Doña Ana again stated that Fray Miguel and Espinosa had told her that Espinosa was her cousin, King Sebastian of Portugal, and that she had been very happy to believe it. There had been no intentional deceit toward the King of Spain on her part. On the contrary, she had expected Philip to be as delighted as she on finding that his nephew was alive. She had only talked to Espinosa at the convent grating, and there was never anything improper about their relationship. She addressed him affectionately, as she believed was her duty, and understood that he wanted to marry her when his peregrinations were over and his kingdom restored. She had not given him her word, saying always that she would not leave the convent without the express permission of Philip II and the Pope; however, she did accept a written marriage pledge from Espinosa in order to obtain his signature and have some proof of his identity. She emphasized again that there existed no plan to abduct her from the convent. Espinosa had gone to Valladolid to get her brother, and the precautions for a secretive return to Madrigal were designed to protect her brother.

This matter of the promise of marriage (*desposorio*) disturbed Philip II greatly and was one of the details which made him suspect that little Clara Eugenia might be Doña Ana's child. Although Doña Ana firmly denied that she planned to leave the convent and marry

Espinosa without her uncle's consent, the other nuns in the convent knew that a marriage vow had been exchanged (*leg.* 173, fols. 249–57), and Doña Ana's servants understood that she planned to be Queen of Portugal some day. One servant said that "la misma doña Ana dixo que tenia sus esperanças en aquel reyno [Portugal] y tambien su estrella en el" (*leg.* 173, f. 236).* Another, although she had not witnessed the *desposorio,* testified that it had taken place at the communion window in the choir. It was this that prompted the king to have Santillán measure the window.

Although both Don Rodrigo de Santillán and Doctor Juan de Llano had decided quite early in the investigation that Fray Miguel was the key figure of the entire matter, there was great delay in focusing attention on the interrogation of Fray Miguel himself. After the interference of Provincial Goldaraz and the appointment of an ecclesiastical judge, Santillán had no authority to question Fray Miguel. The only information Don Rodrigo had been able to obtain was that Fray Miguel believed Espinosa to be Sebastian of Portugal, still alive and wandering in disguise because of a vow made after the Battle of Alcazarquivir. In late October the *alcalde* took Fray Miguel to Medina del Campo for safekeeping until Llano reached Madrigal. Llano arrived in Madrigal on November 15; but the interrogation of the nuns, Doña Ana, and other convent personnel, plus the continued interference of Goldaraz, kept Llano from sending for Fray Miguel until January 15.

Fray Miguel made his first formal confession before Juan de Llano on January 18 (*leg.* 173, f. 227). He had a long time to prepare a version which would protect himself and shift responsibility to Doña Ana and Espinosa. According to Fray Miguel, Doña Ana had requested his appointment as *vicario* of the Madrigal convent because she was interested in Portugal. She was fascinated by the rumors that Sebastian was still alive, keeping a votive lamp burning on the altar for his life and praying often for his return. Although Fray Miguel did not believe the tales about Sebastian, he considered it his duty to entertain Doña Ana with them and to keep her happy. When Gabriel de Espinosa first arrived in Madrigal, pretending that he was Sebastian, Fray Miguel did not believe it, but Espinosa was very clever and finally succeeded in persuading both Fray Miguel and Doña Ana to that belief. Fray Miguel allowed them to talk at the convent grating and knew that they had spoken of marriage. One day Doña Ana persuaded Espinosa to give her a statement which read as follows: "Digo yo Don Sebastian por la gracia de Dios Rey de Portugal que rescibo por mi esposa a la ser^ma doña Ana de Austria hija del ser^mo principe don Juan de Austria por quanto para ello tengo dispensacion de dos sumos pontifices. [signed] Yo el Rey."* When Doña Ana saw the signature, she threw the paper on the ground in anger, saying, "Don Garabato llamo yo esto y no Don Sebastian."* Fray Miguel then returned to his cell, but he believed that they exchanged vows of marriage after his departure. He further testified that he had consented to all this because it made Doña Ana happy and because he really believed that Espinosa was Sebastian. Later he realized his error, but he did not report the matter to the king because he thought that Espinosa would go away after obtaining money and jewels for the alleged purpose of getting Doña Ana's brother.

It was too late for Fray Miguel to shift the blame. In early December Llano and Santillán had decided that the whole plot was engineered by Fray Miguel, and the flimsy explanations given in Fray Miguel's confession of January 18 only served to heighten their conviction. Fray Miguel was much too intelligent a man to be deceived by Espinosa; therefore, the impersonation must have been directed by Fray Miguel. Both judges and Philip II were chafing under the slow pace at which the investigation progressed, and everyone was eager to bring the case to an end. This was the appropriate time to apply torture in the questioning of Fray Miguel and Espinosa.

Before proceeding with the confessions of Fray Miguel and Espinosa which, at last, revealed the truth about what had been going on in Madrigal, let us digress into a matter that evinces the widespread interest in the Madrigal case. In spite of the judges' attempts to conduct their investigations with the utmost secrecy (Don Rodrigo still rejected the services of a scribe when he suspected that the information might deal with the delicate subject of Doña Ana's honor), there was much discussion of the case throughout the surrounding area. The large number of arrests and the involvement of such well known personages as Doña Ana and Fray Miguel could not go unnoticed and without comment.

In early January of 1595, Don Rodrigo was in Medina del Campo at the house of Simón Ruiz when he received an anonymous letter written in a small, neat hand (*leg.* 173, f. 245). Its writer was obviously a well-educated man and probably a clergyman, since he urged the *alcalde* to seek the advice of theologians in his investigations. This particular suggestion was not a welcome one to Santillán who commented to Philip II, "parece que en esto habla como persona sin letras ni sin experiencia que les parece no se puede hazer ni acertar nada sin parecer de theologo y querra ser de la junta de la cual a mi parecer no ay necesidad" (*leg.* 173, f. 119).* The writer offered to furnish valuable aid if Don Rodrigo were receptive to the opinions of others. The sign that he was willing to receive advice was to be his presence at mass the next day in the Church of Sahagún.

Don Rodrigo attended the service specified, and on the following day he received a second letter containing a lengthy account of the unknown writer's opinion about the identity of Gabriel de Espinosa (*leg.* 173, f. 246). The author was surprisingly well-informed about the details and the progress of the investigation, even evincing knowledge of the fact that the king had specifically refused to permit the application of torture in questioning either Fray Miguel or Espinosa. The story being circulated, he said, was that Espinosa was a low-born man who pretended to be Sebastian of Portugal in order to effect his restoration to the throne after the death of Philip II. According to the writer, this could not be possible for many reasons. First, Fray Miguel knew Sebastian too well to be deceived, nor was it conceivable that a man of Fray Miguel's moral stature be party to a plot to place a man of humble birth on the throne of Portugal. It was also common knowledge that Doña Ana thought Espinosa to be her cousin Sebastian and that she had accepted his promise of marriage, a deceit Fray Miguel would not permit if Espinosa were not of royal blood. That Espinosa was really Sebastian, however, did not seem plausible to the anonymous writer. If he were Sebastian, Espinosa would have no reason to wander around Castile in disguise when he would be welcomed by his Portuguese subjects with the greatest joy. In fact, for immediate recognition, he need only present himself to Philip II of Spain. So, if Espinosa was neither a common man nor Sebastian, he must be Dom António, Prior of Crato. This would explain Fray Miguel's position, as well, for Fray Miguel would say that he was Sebastian to protect him. In any event, the writer urged Santillán to proceed with great caution lest the people of Portugal believe their king was being persecuted by the Castilians. It was known that many Portuguese had visited Madrigal during Fray Miguel's residence there, and any misstep on Santillán's part might turn a condition of general unrest into open rebellion.

Unbeknown to the anonymous letter writer, Philip II had given Don Rodrigo permission to use torture in questioning Espinosa on December 15. Although Santillán previously had shown great eagerness to apply torture, he now seemed in no hurry to take advantage of the permission; therefore, Philip repeated it on January 3, this time worded as a command. Santillán's frequent trips between Medina del Campo and Madrigal, the interrogation of other prisoners, and Espinosa's severe illness in late January and early February caused the execution of this order to be delayed until February 27. Meanwhile, the news that the king had consented to the use of torture reached the ears of the anonymous writer, and Don Rodrigo received two more letters in late January, one to be delivered to Juan de Llano in Madrigal. Both letters contained the same message: the writer urged the use of clemency and caution for he was sure that the application of torture in this grave matter would result in a Portuguese rebellion:

Sangre podra v. m. sacar que le pese y que quiça algun dia diera sangre de sus venas por no averla sacado de las agenas. y no querria yo que el negocio viniese a costar mas sangre de la que v. m. pretende sacar. que me temo mucho que la picadura se haze en Madrigal y la sangre ha de saltar en toda Castilla y Portugal. (*leg.* 173, f. 248)

...digo que no son los cordeles los que mas an de apretar este negocio y sacar a luz la verdad. antes tengo gran temor de que la sangre que ellos sacaren ha de ser tierra que la cubra...mas yo acabo con tornar a suplicar a v. m. una y mil veces con el encarecimiento posible que se detenga y advierta que en negocio de esta calidad es mas menester mostrar madureza y sosiego que espiritu de alcalde....* (*leg.* 173, f. 247)

This last comment irritated Santillán who remarked, "muestra ser frayle cuyo voto en las cosas del govierno de las rrepublicas no suele ser muy acertado de ordinario" (*leg.* 173, f. 130).*

While neither the judges nor the king felt that unrest in Portugal had reached such extremes, Llano and Santillán were disturbed by the letters and attempted to identify the writer. The same day that he received the last two letters in Medina del Campo, Santillán discovered a student who had once served in Dom António's household in Portugal. However, the young man had not left his room all that day and further investigation indicated that his handwriting did not match that of the letters nor did he appear to have the intellectual ability necessary to be the anonymous author.

Juan de Llano found a much more likely suspect in the person of Fray Antonio de Sosa, an Augustinian friar of Valladolid and a friend of Provincial Goldaraz. The chief witness of Llano's investigation was a definitor of the Order of Saint Augustine, Fray Juan de Benavente, who had been in contact with both Llano and Santillán since early December concerning Provincial Goldaraz. After the arrival of Juan de Llano in Madrigal, the provincial had shifted his harassing activities from Don Rodrigo to the ecclesiastical judge, charging Llano with interfering with the government of the monastery and enlisting the aid of the papal nuncio in Madrid to keep Llano from entering the convent as frequently as he thought necessary. The provincial's interference enraged Llano as it had Santillán, and Llano was delighted to have such a willing witness against Goldaraz as was Fray Juan de Benavente who had been on bad terms with the provincial for some time.[12] According to Benavente,[13] Goldaraz had been removed from a post in Navarre some years before for being a French sympathizer; and since Goldaraz had been responsible for bringing Fray Miguel dos Santos to Madrigal and keeping him there as *vicario,* Benavente was sure that the provincial and Henry IV of France had a hand in the Madrigal case. In early February Benavente reported that Goldaraz and his friend, Fray Antonio de Sosa, were spreading false information about the Madrigal investigation. Fray Antonio had preached publicly against Espinosa's imprisonment and openly opposed the Crown's policy in Flanders. In Benavente's opinion, Sosa and his inflammatory words were "bastante para lebantar una comunidad" (enough to cause an uprising) (*leg.* 173, f. 129), and something must be done to silence him. A few days later, Juan de Llano showed the anonymous letters to Benavente who identified the handwriting and style as those of Fray Antonio de Sosa. Benavente believed that Provincial Goldaraz was an accomplice in the Madrigal affair and that he probably feared he would be implicated if the prisoners were questioned under torture. He had communicated this fear to his good friend, Fray Antonio, who wrote the letters in an attempt to delay the use of torture. The letters had been delivered in the house of Simón Ruiz, a friend of Fray Antonio, and Benavente further stated, "no se conoce en toda la provincia hombre mas atrevido y precipitado para semejantes cosas que el dicho fray Antonio" (*leg.* 173, f. 244).*

Juan de Llano was in favor of arresting Fray Antonio de Sosa immediately, but Don Rodrigo, who had no desire to get mixed up in "pasiones y rrencores de frayles" (friars' squabbles and feuds) (*leg.* 173, f. 113), was more interested in verifying the connection between Goldaraz and Henry IV of France before taking definite steps against the provincial and his friends. Spain had been at war officially with France since January, and the King of France was protecting and aiding Dom António, Prior of Crato. Philip II and his advisers agreed with Santillán. Cristóbal de Mora believed the letters were written by some crank who warranted no attention (*leg.* 173, f. 289), and Philip II was very skeptical about Benavente's accusation against Sosa. *Leg.* 173, f. 140, bears this marginal note in the king's hand: "lo que parece en esto de Fray Antonio de Sosa que creo que conozco y es muy viejo y mas que yo. no se como siendolo haze tan buena letra."* With the new evidence revealed by questioning Espinosa and Fray Miguel under torture, interest shifted to accomplices in Portugal, and the attempts to identify the anonymous letter writer were abandoned. Fray Miguel's confessions did not implicate Provincial Goldaraz and Llano was too busy with difficulties in the Madrigal convent to pursue the matter further.

For a while, Don Rodrigo thought that he had uncovered a link between Henry of France and the Madrigal case, possibly involving Goldaraz, as well; but the scent proved to be false. It is an interesting side light, however, which indicates the extensive activities being carried on by subversive groups in and outside of Spanish borders. In January the magistrate (*corregidor*) of Olmedo arrested a young man who claimed to be an Augustinian friar although he had no papers to prove it. The prisoner was reported to have come from France, and because he gave his nationality as Portuguese, the *corregidor* suspected that he might have something to do with the Madrigal case. The prisoner was transferred to Medina del Campo where Santillán questioned him on February 10. This time he said that he was Bernardo del Río, a Catalan by birth and a lay brother of the Order of Trinitarians (*leg.* 173, f. 237). He had only pretended to be an Augustinian friar in hope of obtaining freedom through the prior of the Augustinian monastery of Medina del Campo. Although Río disclaimed any knowledge of the Madrigal case, Santillán's suspicions were aroused: the prior of the Medina monastery was a good friend of Goldaraz; Goldaraz was said to have dealings with Henry IV of France; Río was reported to have come from France; hence, Río could be a spy. In any event, lack of credentials and a charge of vagrancy gave Santillán legal grounds for using torture and sending the prisoner to the galleys even if he proved to have no connection with the Madrigal case.

During the month of March, Don Rodrigo was occupied with the interrogations of Espinosa and Fray Miguel; as a consequence, he did not turn his attention to Bernardo del Río until April 7. This time torture was used and the prisoner talked freely, confessing that he was employed by Antonio Pérez, former secretary to Philip II, to carry letters between Pérez and Dom António in southern France and a certain Manuel Mendes in Lisbon. In 1591 Río had been a bandit in the gang hired to rescue Antonio Pérez from jail in Zaragoza. His brave deeds that day attracted the attention of Pérez who took him to southern France where they were given lodging by the sister of Henry IV. Pérez then entered the service of the King of France. According to Río, Pérez and Dom António were planning to assassinate the Viceroy of Catalonia, and Pérez was trying to organize an expedition to attack Navarre where he believed that he had some support. Río still asserted that he knew nothing about the Madrigal case, although he did say that a Portuguese priest had visited him in prison who said that he had been sent by that same Manuel Mendes and other friends of Fray Miguel in Lisbon to find out what was going on in Madrigal (*leg.* 173, fols. 154 and 155).

In spite of Río's connections with Spanish enemies, it was quite evident that there was no link between him and Fray Miguel and/or Provincial Goldaraz. Fray Miguel, questioned under torture on April 20, testified that he did not know Bernardo del Río nor had he been in correspondence with Antonio Pérez (*leg.* 173, fols. 160 and 163). On May 1, however, Fray Miguel named, among other friends of Dom António, a merchant named Manuel Mendes who lived in the Rossio in Lisbon. Don Rodrigo was sure that this was the same Manuel Mendes to whom Río carried mail and he was very eager to have him identified, even suggesting that Río be sent to Lisbon for that purpose (*leg.* 173, f. 171). There was a slight effort made to locate Mendes through Don Juan de Silva, a member of the Council of Portugal; but when Silva reported that there were six or seven merchants by that name, none living in the Rossio (*leg.* 173, f. 202), the investigation was dropped. The king and his other ministers did not share Santillán's interest in Mendes since his connection with the Madrigal case was doubtful. Interest shifted to other more important Portuguese accomplices, and Mendes' only role was to delay the sentencing of Bernardo del Río until August 2. Although no charges had been proven against Río, he was guilty of treason by his own confession. Santillán sentenced him to 200 lashes and ten years in the galleys (*leg.* 173, f. 188).

Let us now return to the information given by Fray Miguel and Espinosa after Philip II had granted permission for them to be questioned with torture. Espinosa was put on the rack in Medina del Campo by Don Rodrigo on February 27, and Doctor Llano administered the same treatment to Fray Miguel in Madrigal on March 1. The information given by the two men under torture was so similar that it had to be the truth—or something very close to it— and it confirmed the innocence of Doña Ana. The methods used by Fray Miguel to convince her of Espinosa's identity as King Sebastian were clever enough to deceive a woman of much greater experience, which fact Llano clearly pointed out to Philip II: ". . . que teniendole como le tenia en tanta opinion, creyendo que no avia mas verdad ni religion de la que el le enseñaba y dezia, no es mucho que la engañase con tales embustes de que ella con el sentimiento y ternura que es razon y mucho por no averlo manifestado a Vª Mᵈ como estaba obligada. y es de estimar que no la engañase en otras cosas que tocaran a la fee como lo an hecho otras personas de menos opinion. de que se deben a dios muchas gracias" (*leg.* 173, f. 17).*

Under torture Fray Miguel confessed that he had persuaded Espinosa to pretend to be Sebastian and that he had tutored Espinosa in what to say to Doña Ana so as to convince her of his identity. In order to further Doña Ana's deception, Fray Miguel had started a year before to tell her of certain revelations that came to him during the divine service of the mass. A heavenly voice told him that Doña Ana was destined to serve God in a much higher office than her present one. Then he saw Jesus Christ hanging on the cross with Doña Ana standing on one side and Sebastian on the other, and God told him that the two were to be united in matrimony to free Jerusalem from the power of Mohammed. Fray Miguel reported many such visions during the next year, all indicating that God desired the union of Doña Ana and Sebastian for His service. Finally, when Espinosa came to Madrigal, Fray Miguel claimed to have seen God's finger over Espinosa's head identifying him as King Sebastian of Portugal (*leg.* 172, f. 96). Once Doña Ana was convinced that Espinosa was Sebastian, Fray Miguel arranged the *desposorio,* although Doña Ana always insisted that she would marry only with the full consent of the Pope and Philip II. Fray Miguel further confessed that with the added prestige of having contracted the marriage of the king's niece, he wrote to many Portuguese nobles in July of 1594, saying that he had found Sebastian still alive and begging for their support. Many answered his letter, indicating that they were overjoyed at the good news and would be delighted to serve the resuscitated king once his identity was established beyond any doubt. The Count of Redondo,[14] one of those receiving Fray Miguel's letters, sent a servant named Francisco Gomes to Madrigal to look at Espinosa. Fray Miguel arranged for Gomes to observe Espinosa from a distance, having warned Espinosa that he was under inspection. Gomes returned to Portugal convinced that King Sebastian was alive and living in Madrigal (*leg.* 173, f. 228).

Espinosa's confessions agreed with those of Fray Miguel in general terms (*leg.* 173, fols. 149, 241, and 242). He had met Fray Miguel in Lisbon during the Portuguese campaign when he was a soldier in the Spanish army and helped defend a monastery against the sacking attempts of some German soldiers. When he came to Madrigal in June, 1594, Fray Miguel recognized him and persuaded him to assume the identity of King Sebastian. The written promise of marriage he gave to Doña Ana had been dictated by Fray Miguel, and Espinosa stated very emphatically that there had never been anything improper in his deportment with Doña Ana. The little girl, Clara Eugenia, was born in Oporto some two years before to Espinosa and Inés Cid, whom he had brought to Madrigal as the child's nursemaid. He could give very little information about the persons to whom Fray Miguel had written because Fray Miguel had not discussed those plans with him in any detail. Fray Miguel had not shown him the letters or mentioned specific names, saying only that he had written to important people in Portugal, Madrid, and Portuguese India that King Sebastian was still alive. Fray Miguel also told Espinosa that the man sent by the Duke of Aveiro and the Count of Redondo had gone back to Portugal very well pleased with what he had seen in Madrigal.

Fray Miguel's list of correspondents included some very important people: the Duke of Aveiro, the Count of Redondo, Rodrigo de Alemcastro (or Lencastre, major-domo to the crown prince and cousin of the Duke and Duchess of Bragança), Fray Manuel da Conceição (Augustinian provincial superior in Portugal), Fray António de Santa Maria (uncle of the Duke of Aveiro), Francisco Mascarenhas,[15] Martim de Alarcão (these last two were in Madrid at the time), Rodrigo de Noronha (president of the Senate of Lisbon), Jorge Barbosa (*alférez* or standard-bearer of Coimbra), Alvaro de Medeiros Bercados (in Évora), and Jorge de Albuquerque (in Goa). Fray Miguel said that he had heard from all but Albuquerque, saying that they were happy to hear the good news. He had also written to the Archbishop of Lisbon asking for money (which was refused) and to António Melo de Castro. The latter answered that he had seen the king so surrounded by the Moors during the battle that it was impossible for him to escape, and he begged Fray Miguel not to bother him with such an absurd idea. Fray Miguel stated that he had sent all these letters to Fray António de Santa Maria in Madrid, who forwarded them on to Lisbon for delivery through Fray Álvaro de Jesús, procurator-general of the Augustinian Order (*leg.* 173, f. 18).

Since all of Fray Miguel's papers had been destroyed before his arrest, there was no way to verify this part of his testimony other than through the people to whom he had written. However, before accusing people of such importance, Philip II wanted to be very sure that Fray Miguel was telling the truth. The priest's astuteness and daring, combined with his desperate position, did not produce a climate of trustworthiness, and the king strongly suspected that he was giving false testimony in an effort to postpone sentence. Llano and Santillán were instructed to co-operate in every possible way, using each prisoner's testimony in the interrogation of the other and questioning them carefully about the accomplices.

On March 20, Fray Miguel further testified that he had really planned to use Espinosa's resemblance to Sebastian in a plot to put Dom António, Prior of Crato, on the throne of Portugal. Espinosa was not aware of this, of course. After the death of Philip II, Fray Miguel intended to present Espinosa as Sebastian and to use the resuscitated king's popularity in re-establishing the political independence of Portugal. Then Espinosa would be exposed as a fraud, and Dom António would replace him as the most acceptable candidate. Fray Miguel also testified that, in order to gain Dom António's approval of this plan, he had written him in July asking him to come to Madrigal. The letter, forwarded through Fray Álvaro de Jesús to Manuel Tavares in Lisbon, reached Dom António when he was going through Galicia en route from England to Portugal. In late August Dom António came to Madrigal in disguise, accompanied by several friends. They stayed some three days in an inn which Fray Miguel could not identify, saw Espinosa without his knowing it, and decided to support Fray Miguel's plan. Dom António did not believe that Espinosa resembled Sebastian greatly, yet he thought the idea had a good chance to succeed and he agreed to spread the news that Sebastian was alive and in Madrigal. All this was accomplished without the knowledge of Doña Ana and Espinosa. Dom António went on to Lisbon, telling Fray Miguel that he could always be reached through Manuel Tavares, a merchant in whose house he stayed while in Lisbon (*leg.* 173, fols. 27 and 229).

This was an important revelation, indeed, for it meant that Dom António was able to travel through Spain and Portugal without detection. However, when ratification of the confession was required, Fray Miguel retracted everything, saying that (because of his fear of torture) he had invented the whole story about writing to the important people and about Dom António's visit to Madrigal. The following day Juan de Llano prepared him for interrogation with torture, and Fray Miguel decided to renew his confession of

March 20. This was the testimony that Fray Miguel repeated during the next month, with and without torture, until investigations made in Portugal forced him to make minor changes.

Through Juan de Silva, Count of Portalegre and member of the Council of Portugal, Philip II ordered the arrest of two Lisbon merchants named by Fray Miguel as succoring Dom António, but neither man could be identified or found. Fray Miguel was questioned again on May 1, and this time he stated that the man in whose house Dom António stayed was António de Fonseca, not Manuel Tavares. He had named Tavares and the other merchant falsely to protect Dom António. The rest of the information given in previous confessions was true, he said, except for three names which he subtracted from his list of correspondents (*leg.* 173, f. 231).

The revised list of names was sent to Juan de Silva who, this time, was able to locate the lawyer, António de Fonseca, and Francisco Gomes, the servant of the Count of Redondo who allegedly made the trip to Madrigal. Juan de Silva, nonetheless, was extremely skeptical of Fray Miguel's information and refused to believe that Dom António had been either in Madrigal or in Lisbon (*leg.* 173, f. 202). This opinion was shared by Philip's other ministers who believed that Fray Miguel's confessions, retractions, and changing of names were all made in an effort to delay punishment. Juan de Llano and Don Rodrigo, on the other hand, did not consider Fray Miguel's contradictions a necessary indication of general prevarication since he had been able to give a reasonable explanation for each one, and they were very anxious to effect the arrest of the Portuguese accomplices named by him.

On May 22 Fray Miguel again ratified the information given on May 1, and the arrests of Fonseca and Gomes were made. The prisoners denied any connection with Fray Miguel and Dom António (*leg.* 173, fols. 55 and 56), but Llano and Santillán were not satisfied with the interrogation. Santillán had questioned two Madrigal innkeepers with whom Francisco Gomes might have stayed when he came to Madrigal; and although they could make no positive identification, they did say that some Portuguese merchants had been in Madrigal in July, asking for directions to the convent (*leg.* 173, f. 175). Santillán and Llano continued to question Fray Miguel, with and without torture, and they were sure that he was telling the truth. The Portuguese officials were not well-informed about the case and could not be expected to conduct a proper interrogation; therefore, the only effective method for getting at the truth would be to have the prisoners brought to Castile where they could be confronted with Fray Miguel, if necessary. Fray Miguel's delaying tactics were quite successful: his first formal confession was taken on January 18; Gomes and Fonseca were not arrested until early June; and in July Philip II ordered Juan de Silva to send the two Portuguese prisoners to Madrid. At the same time, Llano was instructed to finish his investigations at the Madrigal convent and take Fray Miguel to Madrid where he could be questioned with Gomes and Fonseca. It was impossible to accomplish this before the end of August.

Juan de Llano's investigations in Madrigal were encountering a variety of difficulties, and there was reason to believe that the apostolic judge was not conducting himself in a manner completely beyond censure. According to Llano, he had rescued the nuns from the tyranny of Provincial Goldaraz, and they were very grateful to him. Goldaraz was already under suspicion because of his refusal to co-operate with the king's ministers in their investigations and because of his alleged complicity in the anonymous letters; consequently, when Cristóbal de Mora wrote Llano in February that he had heard complaints about Llano's procedures in Madrigal, Llano could easily attribute the complaints to Provincial Goldaraz and his efforts to impede progress of the Madrigal case. Later in the spring, however, complaints from other sources began to cast some doubt on the accuracy of the ecclesiastical judge's reports about what was going on in the convent of Nuestra Señora de Gracia la Real. It seemed that the tyranny of Goldaraz had been replaced by the tyranny of Llano.

Although Llano and Santillán both upheld Doña Ana's innocence in the conspiracy to pass Espinosa off as King Sebastian of Portugal,

Doña Ana did not consider Llano a friend or protector. On October 26, Don Rodrigo had confined Doña Ana to her cell under the guard of four nuns, permitting her to leave only to attend mass. In late March Llano took away that one privilege because she went through the infirmary on her way to mass and spoke to the sick nuns, thereby violating the terms of her imprisonment which prohibited communication with anyone except her guards and the investigating officers. Doña Ana was a proud woman, and the frustration of six months' imprisonment without any direct word from her uncle, plus her own ill health, finally drove her to open rebellion against Llano's treatment. She refused to obey his summons to go to him; and when he came to her cell, harsh words were spoken on both sides. Doña Ana quickly realized, however, that Llano was her only mediator with the king and that her only chance for receiving clemency was dependent on Llano's good will. Swallowing her pride, she wrote him a pitiful letter asking for his mercy and understanding (*leg.* 173, f. 223).

Doña María Belón, one of the guards assigned to Doña Ana by Santillán, was also the object of Llano's wrath because she had encouraged Doña Ana's disobedience by accompanying her to the infirmary. Doña María was confined to her cell at the same time that Doña Ana was prohibited from attending divine services. Like Doña Ana, Doña María wrote to Llano, begging for mercy (*leg.* 173, f. 225); and when their pleas were ignored, both nuns tried to send letters to Don Rodrigo asking him to intercede with Doctor Llano on their behalf. Unfortunately for the two women, the letters fell into the hands of Juan de Llano. On April 5 the apostolic judge formally charged them with breaking the terms of their confinement and spreading gossip about him. Doña María Belón made a public confession of guilt and repentence: "...y ansi pedia perdon a el dicho señor juez ap^tico y a mi el dicho escribano hechandose y prostrandose a sus pies delante del dicho combento y lo mesmo hicieron luego la priora y monjas mas ancianas del dicho combento en nombre de todo el con mucho sentimiento y lagrimas..." (*leg.* 173, f. 258).* In view of the advanced age of Doña María, who had been a nun for forty years, and the station of Doña Ana, who was not forced to make a public statement of contrition, Llano lifted the punishment of excommunication. The nuns and friars of the monastery were charged not to say anything of the matter to anyone outside the convent, and Llano was "persuaded" not to report the incident to the king by several visiting generals of the Augustinian Order who wanted to avoid unfavorable publicity.

Juan de Llano had good reason to be apprehensive about what other people were saying about him. By May, nuns other than Doña Ana were objecting to his high-handed methods, and word of their complaints had reached the court. On June 26 Doña Ana wrote to Philip II and to his *capellán mayor,* García de Loaysa, complaining of Llano's harsh treatment and begging for an impartial judge to hear her confessions (*leg.* 173, fols. 218 and 219). In spite of being warned that he should practise more self-restraint, Llano continued his policy of intimidating the convent congregation with threats of excommunication and prohibiting all contact between the monastery personnel and the outside world. By early July the situation could not be controlled. On July 3 Llano issued an *auto* against the nuns for spreading gossip about convent affairs. The next day the congregation was assembled in the choir by the subprioress—the prioress had refused to come, saying she was ill—to hear the official reading of the *auto.* Llano charged them to come to him for absolution if they fell under its interdictions. He waited in the chapel until dark, but no one came (*leg.* 173, f. 59). The same day the *vicario* of the nuns sent to Madrid a formal memorandum of complaints against Llano.

When Fray Andrés Ortiz came to the Madrigal convent as *vicario* in late May or early June of 1595, he found the nuns so upset over Llano's behavior that he felt it his duty to take some kind of action. On July 4, when Llano was notifying the nuns of their excommunication for having spread gossip, Fray Andrés and the confessor of the nuns, Fray Alonso Rodríguez, called on Don Rodrigo de Santillán who was staying at a Madrigal inn. Don Rodrigo did not want to take a personal part in the matter and suggested that they write to authorities in Madrid. Fray Alonso departed that very day, carrying the memorandum of complaints and letters from the *vicario* to Cristóbal de Mora, García de Loaysa, Rodrigo Vázquez de Arce, president of the Council of Castile, and Fray Enrique Enriques, prior of the Augustinian monastery in Madrid.

The charges against Llano were indeed serious, and Fray Andrés was begging for help in remedying a situation which had grown beyond the control of the prioress and the *vicario*. According to the memorandum (*leg.* 173, f. 391), Juan de Llano and his scribe entered the cloister of the convent every day with no other purpose than to chat with their two "devotas" (devotees) to whom they had given "sayas de tornasol" (iridescent petticoats) in spite of the objections of the prioress and the *vicario*. Llano and his scribe often stayed in the convent until late, talking to the nuns in the dark and refusing to obey the prioress' order to light a candle. Llano took many liberties with the nuns—taking them by the hand, embracing them, and covering them with his cloak—and then prevented them from telling the *vicario* or the friars by threats of excommunication. The memorandum also charged the apostolic judge with treating the nuns like *pícaras* (rogues, scamps), calling them Lutherans and "bellacas desvergonzadas" (shameless scoundrels), excommunicating those who opposed his will, and threatening to turn them over to the Inquisition as heretics. Llano had even suggested to Don Rodrigo that he, too, could have a "devota" and enter the convent if he chose. Don Rodrigo refused.

Juan de Llano was not long in hearing that a formal complaint had been made against him. Although he did not yet know what the charges were, he wrote to Philip II on July 7 saying that they were not true. He had not reported on the difficulties with the nuns before, he said, because he believed that it would only slow down the progress of the "negocio principal," but he promised a full report as soon as possible (*leg.* 173, f. 60). On July 13 Fray Alonso Rodríguez returned from his courier's mission, whereupon Llano's investigation started. Fray Alonso was confined to a monastery on the outskirts of Madrigal without permission to speak to anyone, even the prior, and Fray Andrés was questioned carefully about the contents of the memorandum. Fray Andrés confessed that he had not verified the charges made against Llano, only reporting what the nuns told him. Other than the prioress, he could not identify his informants since he knew few of the nuns by name and had talked to many through a cloth-covered grating without seeing their faces. He stated that he had not meant to harm the ecclesiastical judge or his scribe and that "ha entendido ser contrario a la verdad todo lo conthenido en el dicho memorial y ansi le pidio perdon a el dicho juez ap^tico prostrado de rodillas y dixo que esta presto de darle sobre ello toda la satisfaccion possible..." (*leg.* 173, f. 259).*

But in spite of Fray Andrés' retraction Juan de Llano had gone too far. As soon as the president of the Council of Castile heard about the letters from Fray Andrés, he ordered Santillán to investigate the charge. Although Don Rodrigo had no desire to become involved in ecclesiastical matters and suggested that it would be much more satisfactory if the investigating were done by an official of the Augustinian Order or some other cleric, Philip II ordered the *alcalde* to proceed with the investigation when Llano left Madrigal. On August 2, Santillán reported that he was questioning the oldest and most respected nuns of the convent. In his defense Llano had sent to the king letters signed by nuns, and Santillán discovered that many of those nuns had signed at Llano's request without knowing the contents of the letters (*leg.* 173, fols. 187 and 192).

Unfortunately, the results of Santillán's investigations do not appear in the *proceso* records, and there is no way of knowing what action, if any, was taken against Juan de Llano. The only direct reference Llano made to the charges against him and to Santillán's investigations appears in a letter from Madrid dated August 23 in which he asked that the matter be turned over to the provincial superior of the Order of Saint Augustine. Don Rodrigo's ill health was delaying the matter—he had been bothered with recurrent fevers during the month of August—and it was obviously distasteful to Llano that he be investigated by his former colleague: "...muy en su lugar estaria que se cometiese a otra persona desapasionada que con menos ruydo lo hiziese, y con mas satisfaction de todos para que la verdad clara y abiertamente se supiese, y Su M^d y sus ministros entendiesen quien les a serbido y sirbe con la fidelidad que debe para darles el premio o el castigo" (*leg.* 173, f. 81).*

Before leaving Madrigal to accompany Fray Miguel to Madrid, it was necessary for Juan de Llano to terminate the cases against the other ecclesiastical prisoners in his custody. The principal figure was, of course, Doña Ana de Austria, whose fate would be shared by her two companions and friends, Doña María Nieto and Doña Luisa de Grado. The other friars and nuns imprisoned by Llano for disciplinary reasons were undoubtedly released upon his departure since they were not actually involved in the criminal case, and Llano had already disposed of the two Portuguese confessors of the nuns. Fray Agostinho dos Anjos, who was arrested by Santillán in October, testified that he had been brought to Madrigal by Fray Miguel. Fray Miguel instructed him to tell Doña Ana that King Sebastian was still alive, and when he refused to do so, he was replaced as Doña Ana's confessor by Fray Alonso Rosete, "portugues de pocas letras y de mal juizio,"* according to Fray Juan Benavente (*leg.* 172, f. 61). Fray Alonso arrived in late September, and although he professed to know nothing about what was going on between Doña Ana and Fray Miguel, Llano was sure that he told the nuns Sebastian was still alive. At Llano's insistence, Fray Alonso was transferred to Bilbao in January.

On March 7, immediately after Espinosa and Fray Miguel were first questioned with torture, Juan de Llano closed his case against Doña Ana, sending to the king statements of formal charges against her and his opinion about her punishment (*leg.* 173, f. 13). The charges were threefold: accepting a common man as King Sebastian of Portugal, exchanging a promise of marriage in spite of her profession, and failing to notify the king of these events as was her duty. Llano recommended clemency despite the gravity of the charges, pointing out that her deceit stemmed from the great respect she had for Fray Miguel who was her mentor throughout, that she had been in the convent from such an early age that she could not be expected to understand the consequences of her actions, and that she should be given special consideration because she was the king's niece. At this time Llano did not recommend a specific sentence, leaving that decision to the king and his advisers in Madrid. Throughout the spring Llano continued to request that he be allowed to close the case against the nuns and move with Santillán and the other prisoners to Madrid, where they would not be delayed by the necessity of conferring with His Majesty by mail; but Philip, still not satisfied about the parentage of the little girl, preferred to keep them in Madrigal. The contradictory testimony about Portuguese accomplices and the decision to face Fray Miguel with Francisco Gomes and António de Fonseca at last forced Philip to consent to terminating the investigations in Madrigal; on July 8 he ordered Llano to sentence the three nuns in accordance with the instructions that had been given him.

Formal notification of the charges was made on July 17. The next day Doña Ana wrote to Philip complaining that Llano had not permitted her the services of a *procurador* and *letrado* (that is, legal counsel) for her defense, a privilege granted to all criminals, so she sent her statement directly to the king (*leg.* 173, f. 220). Her pleas for mercy were not heeded. On July 21 formal sentence was passed. Doña Ana was confined to her cell for a period of four years without speaking or communicating with anyone. She would be allowed to attend mass on feast days and was to fast on bread and water every Friday. The sentence stipulated, as well, that she was to be transferred to another convent, stripped of all privileges hitherto enjoyed as a member of the royal family, and prevented from ever holding any office in her order (*leg.* 173, f. 73). Indeed, this was severe punishment. Doña Ana repeated her vain appeals to Philip, also writing to the queen to intercede for her (*leg.* 173, fols. 221 and 222).

It is impossible to determine how much the ill will which had developed between Doña Ana and Juan de Llano influenced the sentence, but it appears that Doña Ana's punishment was determined by Philip himself and that, if it had been left up to the king's ministers, the sentence would have been lighter. Although Llano

Sebastian I, King of Portugal. From the portrait by Christôvão de Moraes in the Muséu Nacional de Arte Antiga, Lisbon.

fuese y al vien de que aui que se diger es dar por
mui dos caualos pedi me mas y deso mas
aguan di yo y es en quien ... me ya ue
de la ... disuer mano y el mas ... de licion
si ... yo que vim a re mi ... que es en de mi
... y ... zedi ... con el ... que y mi
... no me ... ... no ... y no
... me ... que ... si re mi Religion
y ser uas tos ... ... si ... mi yo siempre
... con el ... vi da que no quiero
... ... casa si no ...
... lo que mas me ... y a ... cara
... la ca ... persona de vm ... con
... a mi ... y er yes ... y demas ...
... de vm y ... ... de ... carzel a ...
dignio ...

Doña Ana de Austria by an anonymous artist. Property of the Marqués de Santo Domingo. Formerly in the convent of Nuestra Señora de Gracia, Madrigal.

End of a letter of Doña Ana de Austria to Philip II dated July 18, 1595, after she had been officially notified of the charges brought against her (see p. 88). From the original (*leg.* 173, f. 220) in the Archivo General de Simancas.

Philip II, King of Spain. From the portrait by Juan Pantoja de la Cruz in the Library of the Escorial.

Sentence of Gabriel de Espinosa. Marginal note by Philip II approves minor alterations made in the *pregón* (see p. 94). From the original (*leg.* 173, f. 271) in the Archivo General de Simancas.

Sentencia de Espinosa

En el pleyto q es entre el fiscal d su M.d
actor acusante. y Gabriel de Espinosa
Reo acusado por la culpa q contra el re=
sulta del proceso en esta causa hecho =
fallo q debo condenar y condeno al d.ho
Gabriel de Espinosa a q d la carcel donde
esta preso sea sacado y puesto en un serron
y sea arrastrado en la forma acostum=
brada por las calles publicas acostumbradas
hasta llegar a la plaça donde en una
horca q para el efecto sera fecha
sea ahorcado hasta q naturalmente
muera y quitado d la d.ha horca
sea desquartizado y puesto en quatro
quartos por los q.tro caminos q por
mi fueren señalados y la cabeça d sea
puesta en una jaula de hierro y en
un palo en el lugar q por mi fuere
señalado y por esta mi sentencia
d.f.va

Cabeça d.l Gregor.o

Esta es la Justicia q manda hazer
el Rey n.ro s.or y don P.o de Sanctillan eor
su Juez a este hombre por trayder a su
Religion y haverse fingido q n.o
q.al siendo hombre baxo y embustero.
d.f.

Ruins of the Augustinian convent at Madrigal de las Altas Torres.

Anonymous letter warning Don Rodrigo de Santillán against the use of torture (see p. 73). From the original (*leg.* 173, f. 247) in the Archivo General de Simancas.

Alguna occasion dio v.m. con salida tan repentina de Medina, y mas acal tiempo, de que se entendiese, que mis
cartas le echauan della, por no verme obligado a oyr semejantes auisos alos passados, pero quien conoce a v.m.
y sabe quan aduertido es en todas sus cosas muy seguro estara de que eso aya sido la causa, porque fuera
mucha falta de aduertencia no echar de ver, que por mas experiencia, y prudencia que vno tenga puede
errar, y que para no errar es vnico remedio el oyr, y recevir de buena gana el parecer de otros, que muchos ojos ya sabe v.m. que veen mucho, y que seria algun genero de presumpcion, y arrogancia fiar vno
tanto de lo que los suyos alcançan, que no le pareciese podrian otros alcançar mas, y descubrir la tierra
que el en su vida quiça no descubriera, y si pensara que v.m. coxeaba deste pie, pusierale delante quan
malo era para entrar en negocio tan graue, en que es menester muy particular ayuda de Dios para no hazer un gran borron, y que esta se desmerece tanto por ese camino, que por mas letras, discrecion, y prudencia, y aun por mas sana intencion, que v.m. tenga es mucho de temer suele castigar n̄o Señor con
dexarle hazerse las cosas de suerte que escarmiente para todos los dias de su vida, mas estoy tan ageno
de presumir de v.m. una cosa como esta, y tan cierto de que gusta de ser aduertido en esto, y mas quando en
el acertar, o, errar se interesa tanto, como en la presente ocasion, que si otra cosa no melo impidiera con el
rostro descubierto me fuera a dezirle a v.m. mucho mas delo que le digo por estos rodeos, y ya que esperar
aora no puede ser en prosecucion delo començado añadire aqui algunas breues razones, y todas se resu-
men en suplicar a v.m. que pues asta aqui ha ydo con tanto tiento, y consideracion en este negocio con
lo qual se ha dado una gran satisfacion, de que va bien guiado, y que tendra el fin que se desea, prosi-
ga con ese estilo, que si al mejor tiempo le dexa, y se abalança, y enbia con demasiado apresuramiento
sera como los que muy cansados de nadar, y braçear, se vienen a ahogar en la orilla. Persuadase v.m.
que quien le puso este negocio en las manos sin pensar lo permitira, que cada dia se vaya entendiendo
mas lo que es, y que se descubran mas, y mas los daños, que resultaran, si Dios por su misericordia no
los vbiera atajado por este camino, y aunque v.m. aura ya tocado algunos con las manos eran que
le faltan muchos, y que el tiempo los descubrira si seba por sus pasos contados conforme aloque el orden
natural de los negocios pide, y los encubrira, y echara tierra encima si de otra manera se procede, y ya
vera v.m. por quanto no querria auer sido causa deque ilegara tan pernicia a quedase encubierta, y
quan grauemente culpado quedaria por ello delante de n̄o Señor, y delante delos hombres, y muy en
particular delante de su Mag.d que fuera de ser muy conforme asu gran Christiandad, y prudencia el
yr con mucha consideracion, y tiento en todos los negocios, y mas quando son de esta calidad, el daño que
al oso veria auer nacido, de faltar en esto sus ministros le obligaria a terarse por muy mal seruido de
quien si se abalança, y apresura demasiado es por persuadirse que por esa via le sirue mejor, y les a
mas obligado. Declaro me un poco mas, y digo que no son los cordeles los que mas ande apretar este negocio, y sacar aluz la verdad. antes tengo gran temor deque la sangre, que ellos sacaren, los daños tierra
que la cubra, y el porque digo un poco mas ala larga al Señor Doctor Llanes, que suspendiendo v.m.
se comunican todo lo que toca a este negocio por no cansarles haciendoles saer dos vezes una cosa, dexo de
escriuir aluno lo que escriuio al otro, digo lo particular, que lo general no puede dexar de ser cada uno por
serle el intento, y por lo que alli dige vera v.m. que no pretendo, que no aya tormento a su tiempo, sino se
entienda, que fuera deque en qualquier negocio no parece que es su tiempo asta que intentados los demas
medios no queda otro para inquirir, y sacar de rastro la verdad, en este muy en particular ha lugar

Scribal account of Inés Cid's ratification with torture on July 30, 1595. This page contains the official warning read to the prisoner before the application of torture (see p. 91). The signatures of Don Rodrigo de Santillán and Juan López de Victoria, the scribe, precede the notification. From the original (*leg.* 173, f. 264) in the Archivo General de Simancas.

did not repeat his recommendation for clemency after the opinion of March 7, neither did he complain of Doña Ana to Philip during the time that his own conduct was under attack. It is to Llano's credit that he did not take advantage of the king's persistent attitude of suspicion toward his niece.

Philip's harshness toward Doña Ana is inexplicable. She had been foolish and headstrong, but her intentions were certainly not malicious. One would expect more understanding and compassion from His Catholic Majesty for her unfortunate situation, stemming in large part from Philip's insistence that she stay in the convent and from his neglect in providing for her guidance and protection. It is indeed strange that Philip should permit Fray Miguel dos Santos, a political exile who had been in open support of the king's enemies, to be the spiritual guide of his niece. It even seems that Philip was pleased to use the Madrigal plot as a pretext for Doña Ana's disgrace and to insure her profession as a nun. Philip's primary concern throughout was the possibility that little Clara Eugenia might be Doña Ana's daughter; he cared nothing about Doña Ana herself. He refused to acknowledge her frantic pleas for help and seldom even referred to her in his dispatches to the two judges, speaking only of "the nuns."

Two days after passing sentence on Doña Ana and her friends, Juan de Llano left for Madrid, and Philip instructed the provincial of the Augustinian Order, Fray Pedro Manrique, to carry out the sentence. On September 8 Doña Ana was sent to a convent at Avila, accompanied by three priests, a nun, a lay sister, and one servant. "Doña Ana recibio asperamente al principio esta resolucion," reported Provincial Manrique, "despues dio en la cuenta y la llevo con buen animo y confio en dios que con tan justificado escarmiento la a de dar buena de si" (*leg.* 173, f. 95).* Perhaps Doña Ana realized that her punishment could have been more severe, since Doña María Nieto and Doña Luisa de Grado were sentenced to be placed in separate convents and confined for a period of eight years, twice as long as Doña Ana. These two nuns, sisters, were Doña Ana's constant companions and friends. Instead of opening her eyes to the dangers of dealing with Espinosa and believing Fray Miguel, they had taken an active part as "medianeras" and "terceras" (mediators, go-betweens); therefore, they were considered responsible for Doña Ana's actions (*leg.* 173, fols. 14 and 74).

The conclusion of the three nuns' story has a few cheerful details, however. Blas Nieto, servant to Doña Ana and brother to Doña María and Doña Luisa, was acquitted by Don Rodrigo on July 28. He had been in Madrid during the time of Espinosa's stay in Madrigal and knew nothing of his sisters' activities (*leg.* 173, f. 270). Philip III, who succeeded his father in 1598, was much more kindly disposed toward the illegitimate branch of the House of Austria. Doña Ana was restored to royal favor and in 1610 became perpetual abbess of the convent of Las Huelgas in Burgos. Documents pertaining to her appointment are to be found in the Archivo General de Simancas, Sección del Estado, *legajos,* 2994, 991, 993, and 1001.

Don Rodrigo de Santillán was also completing his investigation with the lay prisoners. As well as the *preso principal,* Gabriel de Espinosa, Santillán was holding Juan de Roderos, Inés Cid, Manuel Mendes, and Blas Nieto in Madrigal and three other prisoners in Medina del Campo who proved to have no connection with the Madrigal case. After Espinosa's confessions with torture in March, Santillán believed that he had told all he knew about Fray Miguel's activities; consequently, emphasis shifted from Espinosa to the Portuguese accomplices. Philip II was still determined to verify "lo de la niña," so all formal action against the lay prisoners was postponed until Inés Cid could be questioned with torture after the birth of her child in early June.

On July 8 Philip ordered Santillán to sentence all prisoners in his care after he had again questioned Espinosa and Inés Cid about the origin of little Clara Eugenia. On July 21, 30, and 31 (*leg.* 173, fols. 263, 264, 189) Espinosa and Inés Cid confirmed, with and without torture, the information they had given earlier: that the child was theirs, born in Oporto in the fall of 1592. Inés Cid repeated that she had met Espinosa in Orense in 1591 and had traveled with him through Portugal, Galicia, and Castile. She had

consented to lie at first about the child's origin—that she had
received the baby when it was six months old—only because Espinosa
feared they would be prosecuted for illegal cohabitation if the truth
were known. The scribal account of the ratification with torture
of Inés Cid's confession gives a vivid picture of sixteenth-century
juridical procedures:

Requerimiento   Luego yncontinente visto lo susodicho por el dicho
señor alcalde por ante mi el dicho escrivano, requirio a la dicha Ynes
Cid una, dos y tres vezes y las que de derecho son necesarias que diga la
verdad de lo que save y pasa en este casso con aperzevimiento que si en
el dicho tormento ojo se le saltare, pierna o braço se le quebrare, o en el
muriere, sea por su culpa, quenta y cargo y no del dicho señor alcalde.
por la qual oydo y entiendido dixo que no save ni tiene mas que dezir de
lo que dicho y declarado tiene. y esto dio por su respuesta siendo testigos
los dichos.

ante mi
[signed]   Joan Lopez de Victoria*

Tormento   E luego yncontinente visto lo susodicho por el dicho
señor alcalde, mando a los dichos Pedro de Segovia y Juan Sanchez pre-
goneros de Valladolid hagan su officio y den el dicho tormento a la
dicha Ynes Cid. por los quales fue desnuda en carnes y con unos pañetes
puestos fue ligada a dos aldavas con una cincha por debajo de los braços
y començada a dar la manquerda desde una hasta quince bueltas a los
braços en las quales dezia, Jesus, ay, que me matan, nuestra señora del
Canto, nuestra señora de Guadalupe, bien sabeis bos la verdad que no se
mas de lo que tengo dicho, madre de dios, aved piedad de mi, madre de
dios de consolacion que me matan, ay mi dios, señor alcalde, aya misericordia de mi que no se otra cossa que dezir para el passo en que estoy, ay
mi dios sea conmigo, desbenturada, llena de p[ecad]os, bien saveis bos
que he cometido otros y en esto no bos he ofendido ni se otra cossa mas
de lo que dicho tengo. valgame dios que me matan. que a de ser de mi,
morir, ay traidor, que yo no savia de tus enbustes. y visto por el dicho
señor alcalde lo susodicho y que no decia mas de lo que dicho tiene, la
mando quitar de la dicha mancuerda y que la tendiesen en el potro
adonde fue puesta y dadas las bueltas de cordeles y garrotes de la forma
acostumbrada. y aviendole dado algunas bueltas dellos dezia, madre de
dios del Rosario, que no se mas de lo que dicho tengo. señor alcalde, por
amor de dios que me lean lo que tengo dicho en mis confesiones y la
postrera que me tomo en esta villa delante del doctor Llanos que yo dire

si supiere deso mas que dezir. que la niña es mi hija y la pari donde
tengo dicho y de los quentos y enbustes Despinossa no se mas de lo que
tengo dicho ni destos negocios. y bisto por el dicho señor alcalde, mando
a mi el dicho escrivano le lea las dichas confesiones que fechas tiene. y
por mi el dicho escrivano le fueron leydas. y oydas por ella dixo que para
el passo en que esta que no tiene otra cossa que dezir mas de lo que
dicho y declarado tiene en las dichas confesiones, lo qual todo es la
verdad y lo que save y passa para el juramento que en ellas y en esto
tiene fecho. . . . y declaro ser de la hedad que dicha tiene y no lo firmo
por no saver. y el dicho señor alcalde lo firmo de su nombre.

[signed]   licenciado don Rodrigo de Santillán
Passo ante mi
[signed]   Joan Lopez de Victoria*
(*leg.* 173, f. 264)

Of the lay prisoners sentenced by Don Rodrigo on July 28, only
Blas Nieto and Doctor Manuel Mendes were absolved of all guilt
and released. Both had been arrested by Santillán in October; but
since their innocence was established quite early, it is probable that
they were not kept in confinement during the entire nine months.

Manuel Mendes, not to be confused with the merchant named by
Bernardo del Río as the correspondent of Antonio Pérez, was a
Portuguese doctor who had known Fray Miguel dos Santos years
before in Coimbra. The two men were not close friends and seldom
saw each other; however, when Mendes wrote to Fray Miguel
asking if the friar could arrange a place in Castile for him to
practice, Fray Miguel was delighted to accommodate him, urging
him to come to Madrigal. Mendes was reported to have treated
the wounds of King Sebastian in Portugal after the Battle of
Alcazarquivir, and Fray Miguel hoped to use this reputation to
his own advantage. According to Mendes, a few months after the
disastrous defeat in Africa, he was commissioned to administer
to a wounded man by Francisca Calva, widow of Cristóvão de
Távora.[16] The patient lay in a hut in the mountains near Guimarães
and was attended by four men, all Portuguese, unknown to Mendes.
Mendes treated the wounded man for a week, during which time

the patient kept his face covered with a mask and seldom spoke. Francisca Calva did not tell the doctor who he was, but she gave Mendes the distinct impression that he was King Sebastian. The story got out somehow, and the news circulated that Mendes had cured the king. Mendes testified that he believed Sebastian was dead—that his patient was not the king—and that he had repeatedly informed Doña Ana and Fray Miguel of this opinion. When Gabriel de Espinosa came to Madrigal, Mendes recognized him as a charlatan and warned Fray Miguel to be careful of his friendship. Mendes' refusal to say that Espinosa looked like Sebastian angered Doña Ana who insisted, "soys tan vanos los portugueses que por verle en este traje no le quereys reconocer. no tengays miedo de dezirlo que por esto no os vendra mal ninguno sino mucho bien" (Mendes' confession, *leg.* 173, f. 226).* Seeing that Doña Ana and Fray Miguel treated Espinosa with great honor, Mendes gradually withdrew from his friendship with Fray Miguel. The doctor's testimony was corroborated by Fray Miguel, and he was cleared of suspicion.

The case of Juan de Roderos, servant of Doña Ana and Fray Miguel, is a pitiful one. Although he was not an active participant in the plot, he was aware of the fact that Fray Miguel believed Espinosa to be King Sebastian of Portugal and that Doña Ana treated Espinosa with great respect. When she heard of Espinosa's arrest, Doña Ana sent Roderos to her grandmother, Barbara Blamberg, in Colindres so that Santillán could not question him. Nevertheless, Barbara Blamberg had heard something about the arrest of a man whose name was linked with Doña Ana, and she considered it her duty to advise Junco de Posada of Roderos' whereabouts (*leg.* 172, f. 165). Roderos was arrested and taken to Medina del Campo for interrogation. Although he could add no information to that already obtained from other prisoners, his passive acceptance of the actions of his employers and his attempt to escape apprehension—even though it had been at Doña Ana's orders—made him party to the crime of treason. On July 28, Roderos was sentenced to serve in the galleys for four years (*leg.* 173, f. 270). At Santillán's suggestion, however, the sentence was changed to exile since Roderos had lost the use of both arms in the course of questioning under torture and would be of no use as a galley slave (*leg.* 173, f. 187).

Inés Cid was sentenced to 200 lashes and ten years' exile from Castile and Portugal. She was not an active participant in the conspiracy; still, she had been Espinosa's mistress and had aided him in the fabrication of his royal identity, pretending to be little Clara Eugenia's nursemaid so that Espinosa could say that her mother was a noble lady of Oporto (*leg.* 173, f. 270).

The most severe punishment was reserved for Gabriel de Espinosa who was convicted of lese majesty *in primo capite* for his role as King Sebastian. On July 28 he was notified of his ghastly sentence: to be hanged and quartered, the quarters scattered along the public highways, and his head exhibited in an iron cage:

Sentencia de Espinosa

en el pleito que es entre el fiscal de Su M^d actor acusante y Gabriel de Espinosa reo acusado por la culpa que contra el resulta del processo en esta causa fecho, fallo que debo condenar y condeno al dicho Gabriel de Espinosa a que de la carcel donde esta preso sea sacado, puesto en un seron y sea arrastrado en la forma acostumbrada por las calles publicas acostumbradas hasta llegar a la plaça donde en una horca que para este effecto sera fecha sea ahorcado hasta que naturalmente muera y quitado de la horca sea desquartizado y puesto en quatro quartos por los caminos que por mi fueren señalados y la cabeça sea puesta en una jaula de hierro y en un palo en el lugar que por mi fuere señalado que por esta mi sentencia.* (*leg.* 173, f. 270)

At first Espinosa complained bitterly about the severity of his punishment, requesting legal counsel for an appeal; but the officials assured him that the sentence had been passed with the full knowledge and consent of the king so that he had no choice but to accept it and prepare for execution.[17] Don Rodrigo gave Espinosa an additional day—four days between notification of sentence and execution instead of three—and provided ample spiritual counsel for a complete *descargo de conciencia,* but Espinosa recovered enough of his former spirit and daring to cause the priests some difficulty. His first confessor was a Jesuit, Father Juan de Fuensalida, who was easily impressed by Espinosa's grand manner and pregnant insinuations. Espinosa's principal complaint to Fuensalida was not the sentence of death but the disgraceful manner in which he was to die; and although he never admitted any other identity than that of Gabriel de Espinosa, the way in which he talked about himself led the priest to believe that he was some other person. Fuensalida was not so naive as to believe that Espinosa was Sebastian; however, he did consider Espinosa to be a man "de ingenio y astuto...de grandes fuerças y maior animo...[que] tenia partes y valor para qualquier grande hecho" (*leg.* 173, f. 194).* Don Rodrigo was in no mood to hear all of Espinosa's veiled threats and mysterious hints; consequently, he replaced Fuensalida with two discalced friars and gave orders that he would receive no messages or news from Espinosa. The case was closed, and the priests' only duty was to attend Espinosa's spiritual health.

The *descalzos* had little more success with Espinosa than Fuensalida, and on the day scheduled for the execution they begged Don Rodrigo to delay Espinosa's death because he still refused to demonstrate enough repentance to insure the salvation of his soul. This was Espinosa's only hope. As long as he could find a sympathetic ear, he spread doubt and contradictions.

The following comments are representative of those reported by the priests, *descalzos* and Jesuits, who were with Espinosa: "Mire v. paternidad, yo no naci para principe ni para rey sino para mas que emperador que en medio de mis trabajos siempre e sido hombre honrrado....mucho me espanto que gente de entendimiento viendo las cosas que en mi a avido se persuadan que naci en las malvas. son por ventura cosas las mias de hombre comun y baja. avia de ser yo tan descaminado que emprendiera cosa tan grande tan sin fundamento como dicen. mi muerte descubrira quien yo soy y lo que en esto ay. y lo que yo siento mas que mi muerte es el daño que se a de seguir" (*leg.* 173, f. 194).* When he saw the arrival of an official from Medina del Campo who was dressed in traveling clothes, he cried, "Este cavallero envia el rrey para que me rreconosca

...decid al rrey de la suerte que don Rodrigo trata su sangre" (*leg.* 173, f. 190).* But Don Rodrigo refused to delay any longer and ordered the completion of Espinosa's sentence.

At four o'clock in the afternoon of August 1, 1595, Espinosa was taken from his prison cell and placed in the *serón* (a large basket-like vehicle used to convey prisoners to the gallows) for the ride to the plaza where the gallows awaited him. As the procession passed through the streets of Madrigal, the *pregonero* (crier) announced his crime: "Esta es la justicia que manda hazer el rey nuestro señor y don Rodrigo de Sanctillan en su nombre a este hombre por traydor a Su M^d y haverse fingido persona real siendo hombre baxo y embustero" (*leg.* 173, f. 271). Espinosa punctuated the cry with low comments of "No hay tal" and "Dios lo sabe."* The execution had attracted a large crowd that filled the square and the surrounding streets, and Espinosa, according to Don Rodrigo, surveyed that multitude as if he were about to receive a decoration or some honor. He knelt with the priests at the foot of the gallows for a moment; then mounted the steps. When the rope was already adjusted, Espinosa spied Don Rodrigo de Santillán, who was standing at the window of a house nearby, and called to him with some show of anger, "O señor don Rodrigo! O señor don Rodrigo!" The discalced friar put a crucifix to his lips with the admonition, "Que es esto hermano. Jesús sea con el que le queria."* Espinosa answered, "Pedille perdon," and the hangman carried out his duty.

So died Gabriel de Espinosa, taking the secret of his true identity with him. Up until the very end he refused to give any other name although he repeatedly hinted that he was more than a humble pastry-maker and cook. The two judges—and presumably Philip II, as well—had decided that he was a homeless adventurer who was "hechado a la puerta de la yglesia" (abandoned at the church door) in Toledo and who had never known his parents. It was this ano-nymity which made Espinosa so valuable to Fray Miguel dos Santos. He could claim to be whomever he chose, and no one could prove that he was or was not Gabriel de Espinosa. His activities of the past few years could be verified but not his true origin. He had met Fray Miguel when he was a soldier in Portugal and had evidently learned to speak French and German while traveling in those countries, but his activities prior to 1581 remained unknown. There is, of course, a possibility that his true name was not Gabriel de Espinosa, that his birth was not as humble as that ascribed to him. Perhaps he was the rakehell younger son of some noble family who was fleeing from the consequences of an earlier crime and who preferred death under the name of Gabriel de Espinosa to the dishonor exposure would bring upon his family. One can only conjecture, in any event. We are free to imagine what we will about the mysterious man—base adventurer or noble in disguise—whose death extinguished the flash of hope in many a Portuguese patriot's breast.

Fray Miguel dos Santos was the only prisoner left to be sentenced, but there also remained the matter of the Portuguese accomplices to be clarified before the case against him could be terminated. After passing sentence on Doña Ana and her two friends on July 21, the ecclesiastical judge, Juan de Llano, was then free to escort Fray Miguel to Madrid for questioning with Francisco Gomes and António de Fonseca, who were being transferred from Lisbon. Llano and Fray Miguel left Madrigal on July 23, spending almost a week in Galapagar, just outside Madrid, until arrangements were made for Llano to report to Rodrigo Vázquez de Arce, the president of the Council of Castile, for the disposition of his prisoner.

By August 22 the Portuguese prisoners had also reached Madrid, and they were questioned on August 28 by the *alcalde* Diego de Canal with the assistance of Juan de Llano. Both Fonseca and Gomes repeated the testimony they had given earlier in Lisbon: neither knew why he had been arrested and brought to Madrid; both had known Fray Miguel in the past but had not corresponded with him; Fonseca denied any connection with Dom António, Prior of Crato; and Gomes said he had been in Redondo, not Madrigal, in July of 1594 (*leg.* 173, fols. 268 and 269).

The next day Canal brought his two prisoners to the house where Fray Miguel was confined so that all three prisoners could be questioned together. As a preliminary to the confrontation, Juan de Llano informed Fray Miguel that the Portuguese prisoners continued to deny their culpability and admonished him to tell the truth, whereupon Fray Miguel again retracted everything he had said about the Portuguese accomplices. He had invented the story about writing to important Portuguese, about Gomes' trip to Madrigal, and about Dom António's staying in Fonseca's house. Dom António had not come to Madrigal nor had Fray Miguel even written him about Espinosa. Fray Miguel confessed that he had fabricated all this information to avoid the continued application of torture (*leg.* 173, f. 86).

This was precisely what Fray Miguel had done on March 21 when he retracted his previous confession about the Portuguese accomplices, but he later reinstated the information under torture. There seemed little profit in repeating this same performance in Madrid; if he were put to torture again, he would undoubtedly return to the false testimony. Llano suggested that investigations be made in Redondo to see if Gomes really had been there in July of 1594 and that Fray Alvaro de Jesús, procurator-general of the Augustinian Order, through whom Fray Miguel said that he sent the letters, be questioned. It is very strange that these two obvious inquiries had not been made already—surely that would have been easier than transporting Gomes and Fonseca to Madrid—but Philip II was sure from the beginning that Fray Miguel was giving false testimony. This last retraction confirmed the king's opinion in his own eyes, and he would delay no longer. On September 2, Philip ordered Vázquez to proceed with Fray Miguel's sentence and the release of the Portuguese prisoners immediately following their confrontation.

All three prisoners were questioned together on September 4 with no other result than the confirmation of Fray Miguel's retraction and the innocence of Gomes and Fonseca (*leg.* 173, fols. 88 and 89). *Alcalde* Canal reported that their surprise was quite genuine upon learning why they had been arrested, and he considered their reaction further proof that they were free of all complicity. Since they had been imprisoned for three months without cause, Canal requested that they be allowed to return to their houses without delay and be given financial compensation for the physical discomfort and expenses of imprisonment if Fray Miguel's estate could provide funds (*leg.* 173, f. 384).

On September 6 Llano submitted to the king his statement of formal charges against Fray Miguel and his opinion on the sentence to be passed. As in the case of Gabriel de Espinosa, Fray Miguel's crime was that of treason in the first degree. Although the treacherous plot had been foiled before it could be carried out, Fray Miguel had conspired to overthrow Spanish authority in Portugal by persuading the Portuguese people that Gabriel de Espinosa was their dead king, Sebastian. To further this plan, he had deceitfully persuaded Doña Ana de Austria to this belief and had arranged a promise of marriage between Doña Ana and Espinosa in spite of Doña Ana's status as a professed nun. Ecclesiastical law does not provide for a death penalty in cases not pertaining to faith, no matter what the crime; therefore, Llano recommended that Fray Miguel be unfrocked and handed over to the secular authorities for capital punishment (*leg.* 173, f. 383).

The termination of the *proceso* against Fray Miguel was delayed some six additional weeks, and Llano had some difficulty finding an archbishop who was willing to officiate at the degradation ceremony. Finally, on Monday, October 16, Fray Miguel was officially notified of his sentence, and the degradation took place on the same day in the main chapel of San Martín Church in Madrid with the Archbishop of Oristán officiating (*leg.* 173, fols. 108 and 109). Fray Miguel was stripped of all privileges pertaining to the ecclesiastical status, his habit was exchanged for secular clothing, and he was delivered to Diego de la Canal as a civil prisoner. Three days later the *alcalde*'s sentence was carried out. At noon, October 19, Fray Miguel dos Santos was led through the streets of Madrid to his death on the gallows, and the next day his head was sent to Madrigal for display in the square of that town.

There was little of note surrounding Fray Miguel's death. He gave no further information during the last days, giving himself over entirely to the task of his spiritual salvation. He maintained to the end that he was dying without just cause and restated on the steps of the gallows that the testimony he had given under torture was false. Both the unfrocking and the execution were witnessed by a large number of people, much to Llano's satisfaction because he believed that the public castigation of Fray Miguel was the most effective means of stifling any disturbances which might have resulted from Fray Miguel's subversive activities. "Y con esto acabo sus dias," Llano reported to Cristóbal de Mora, "y con ellos este negocio que tanto fastidio a dado a su M^d y a V^a S^a y a todo el mundo" (*leg.* 173, f. 112).*

V

THE BRIDGE
BETWEEN
HISTORY AND
LITERATURE

*T*he mystery surrounding the person of Gabriel de Espinosa—his equivocal answers, his pretentious manners, and the fact that his true identity had not been clearly established—undoubtedly caused much local comment despite the secrecy with which the investigations were conducted. Moreover, the roles played by Fray Miguel dos Santos and Doña Ana de Austria, both well-known people, made the Madrigal incident too attractive to fall into oblivion. The anonymous letters received by Don Rodrigo de Santillán offer clear evidence of the interest in the arrests, interrogations, and progress of the case that existed among the inhabitants of Madrigal, Medina del Campo, and Valladolid; and the executions of Espinosa and Fray Miguel drew large crowds. Incidents which arouse great public interest generally produce accounts written by eyewitnesses who are eager to give a factual relation and combat the exaggerated tales spread by gossip. In the Madrigal case, the eyewitness was unusually prompt; the first *Historia de Gabriel de Espinosa* appeared in 1595, the same year in which its protagonist was executed for treason.

Unfortunately, there are no extant copies of the first edition of this work, and bibliographical information is quite contradictory. George Ticknor, in *History of Spanish Literature,* 4th ed. (Boston, 1872), III, 10, note 19, cites *A History of Gabriel de Espinosa, the Pastry-cook of Madrigal, Who Pretended to Be King Don Sebastian of Portugal* (title translated from the Spanish) which was published in Cádiz in 1595. In *Fuentes de la historia española e hispano-americana,* 3ª ed. (Madrid, 1952), II, 200, Benito Sánchez Alonso states that the first edition came out in Madrid in 1595 or 1596. Other bibliographers refer to Ticknor's entry. Palau y Dulcet and Salvá list a reprinting of the work in the early seventeenth century, without date or place.[1] The edition which seems to have had the widest circulation and which was consulted for this study was printed in Jerez, 1683, under the title of *Historia de Gabriel de Espinosa, Pastelero en Madrigal, que fingió ser el rey Don Sebastian de Portugal. y assimismo la de Fray Miguel de los Santos, en el año de 1595.* Palau y Dulcet also lists a printing of the same title in Tarragona, 1683; however, it is likely that an error resulted from the name of the printer in Jerez, Juan Antonio de Taragona, and that this edition does not exist.

The *Historia de Gabriel de Espinosa* was published as an anonymous work; nevertheless, there exists in the Library of the Escorial a manuscript (Z-IV-2), very similar to the published *Historia,* which is attributed to a Jesuit priest, Fernando de la Cerda.[2] Biographical data about Father Cerda is not available and little information about the author can be gleaned from the manuscript or the *proceso* documents. The manuscript of sixty-eight folios is written in a clear hand of the late sixteenth or early seventeenth centuries, and its parchment title page presents the following scant information: "Tratado del Suceso del fingido Rey Don Sebastian del qual hasta oy se supo, que hombre era escrito por un Padre de la Compañía." In the prologue the author expresses the desire to correct the many inaccurate versions being circulated. He was an eyewitness to the major part of the events, he says, and had information from dependable eyewitnesses about those events he did not know personally. Although this may be a slight exaggeration on his part, it is true that the author had access to some of the *proceso* documents which he reproduces quite accurately, and, on the whole, his narration agrees with the account which was reconstructed from the *proceso* in the preceding chapter. The moralizing tone of the manuscript and the amount of space devoted to conversations between Espinosa and his spiritual advisers concerning the salvation of his soul immediately preceding his execution indicate that the author was indeed a priest.

The only Jesuit identified by name in the *proceso* was Father Juan de Fuensalida who cared for Espinosa's spiritual health until Santillán replaced him with two discalced friars. The account of Espinosa's last hours given in the Escorial manuscript agrees in large part with the report sent by Fuensalida to Philip II; however, Fuensalida could not have been the author of the manuscript since he had been sent to the province only recently and was not familiar with the earlier stages of the investigation. The author of the manuscript states that he went to Madrigal from Medina del Campo with a "padre de la compañía" to console Espinosa and witness the execution. The priest accompanying him talked to Espinosa alone the morning of the execution and found that Espinosa continued to be unrepentant, refusing to believe that he was to die. Acting on the Jesuit's advice, Santillán had the *serón* brought out and ordered Espinosa tied as if he were to be taken out for immediate execution in order to impress him with the necessity of complete repentance and confession (f. 61ᵛ). According to Fuensalida, a Jesuit official talked to Espinosa that morning and told Santillán that the prisoner was not yet spiritually prepared for death, thereby prompting Santillán to bring out the *serón*. In his letters, Santillán stated that he forbade Father Fuensalida to talk to Espinosa during the last two days. The discalced friars in charge of Espinosa's spiritual health asked that the execution be delayed, but Santillán refused. No reference is made by Santillán to the *serón* incident or to any other Jesuit or Jesuits, although both Fuensalida and the Escorial manuscript say that a "padre de la compañía" accompanied Espinosa to the scaffold along with the *descalzos*. The author of the Escorial manuscript makes several other personal references indicating that he was in Medina del Campo during the course of the investigations. When Espinosa's dyed hair and beard were cut off, the author states that he looked "mas de 55 y aun a mi parezer (in my opinion) de

60 anos" (f. 39ʳ). After Espinosa's death, the *ama* (the nursemaid of the *proceso,* Inés Cid) came through Medina with the two children at which time "vimos" (we saw) the birthmarks on the baby (f. 63ʳ). In the Jerez edition, all these personal references are changed to impersonal statements. By his own statement, the author of the manuscript was not present at Fray Miguel's degradation and execution in Madrid. If it could be established that Father Cerda was or was not at Medina del Campo in 1594–95, it would aid in determining who was the author of the Escorial manuscript and, hence, the Jerez edition of the *Historia.*

The Jerez edition is a reprinting of the Escorial manuscript in revised form. Although the chapter headings are not identical, the division of material is the same with one exception: the Escorial manuscript gives Fray Miguel's letter to Espinosa as a separate chapter, Chapter ii, while the Jerez edition includes the letter in Chapter i. As a consequence, the manuscript contains a total of eighteen chapters and the Jerez edition has seventeen. Basically, the texts are the same. The Jerez edition reproduces the manuscript verbatim in some sections, summarizes or omits passages in others.

The details of the manuscript are generally more accurate than those of the edition. For example, the Jerez edition gives the year of Espinosa's arrest as 1595 (p. 2) and the date of Doña Ana's sentence as July 24 (p. 46), while the Escorial manuscript gives the correct dates, 1594 and July 21 (fols. 1ᵛ and 51ᵛ). In other instances, in the Jerez edition, faulty copying or poor editing has completely destroyed the meaning of the original sentence. When the *ama* gave birth to a little boy in prison, the edition makes the following enigmatic statement: "...bella criatura, tan parecida à la ama, que confirmò ser tambien su madre: con que con esto se deshizo todo lo que Espinosa avia implorado de ser de una señora principal..." (p. 44).* The meaning in the manuscript is quite clear: "...parió un niño, bella criatura, tan parecido a la niña, de suerte que aunque quissieran no pudieran negar que avian salido de una turquesa con lo qual se acavo de declarar del todo que aquella mujer era madre de la niña y que era ficion lo que Espinosa avia dicho que era hija de una mujer principal ..." (f. 50ʳ).*

The Escorial manuscript seems to be a copy and not the original. Occasionally the manuscript text is in error while the Jerez edition has copied the item correctly, indicating that the edition was prepared from still another manuscript. The most glaring example of error in the Escorial manuscript appears in the text of the third anonymous letter found by Don Rodrigo in Medina. The manuscript has displaced a long stretch of material, omitting it from folio 34ʳ and inserting it in folios 34ᵛ–35ᵛ. The Jerez edition (p. 35) preserves the proper sequence; however, the text of the letter is condensed more than that given in the manuscript. The original letter, found among the *proceso* documents, is not arranged so that a page might have been copied in incorrect sequence; therefore, the manuscript was made from a copy of the letter, not the original.

The *proceso* documents were not used by writers of the eighteenth and nineteenth centuries, but they were familiar with one or more of the editions of the *Historia de Gabriel de Espinosa*. This slim little book served as the historical source for the *pastelero* incident, and one can trace the complicated plots of later literary works back to some detail of testimony in the brief *Historia*. The *Historia* itself is not completely objective and factual. Its author reproduces many "facts" about Gabriel de Espinosa which probably circulated at the time of his imprisonment but which do not appear in the *proceso* papers. They may have had a factual basis, but they were exaggerated and distorted by retelling. The information contained in the *Historia* which cannot be corroborated by the *proceso* often has great appeal to the imagination and was utilized to a large extent by later writers.

First, one must become acquainted with the narration of the *Historia* itself. Since the Jerez edition (and, presumably, the two earlier editions) is based on the Escorial manuscript, a summary of the manuscript will be used as the oldest and most reliable version

*Translations of starred passages may be found in Appendix B.

of the story of Gabriel de Espinosa as it was first presented to the
reading public of Spain. Variations between the Escorial manuscript
and the Jerez edition will be indicated.

Chapter i (fols. 1ᵛ–3ᵛ) relates the arrest of Gabriel de Espinosa
in Valladolid much as Don Rodrigo reported the event to Philip II.
A "mujercilla" denounced Espinosa to the authorities as a thief, and
Don Rodrigo found valuable jewels in his possession: a unicorn cup,
a gold book, a ring with the king's likeness, and some religious
images. Espinosa was wearing underclothes of fine cloth; and although he claimed to be a pastry-cook in the service of Doña Ana de
Austria, his manner of words aroused the *alcalde's* suspicions. After
taking Espinosa to jail, Don Rodrigo sent a letter to Doña Ana,
asking her to identify Espinosa; but before her answer arrived, a
messenger was apprehended carrying letters to Espinosa from Doña
Ana and Fray Miguel.

Chapter ii (fols. 3ᵛ–5ᵛ) gives the first letter from Fray Miguel, an
accurate copy of the *proceso* document except for three omissions
which deal with Doña Ana. This letter assumed great importance
in the plots of later literary works because of the details concerning
plans for Espinosa's return in disguise to Madrigal and references
to those who were to accompany him.

Chapter iii (fols. 5ᵛ–8ᵛ) relates the initial stages of the investigation. Santillán sent Espinosa to Medina del Campo and went
himself to Madrigal where he arrested Doña Ana and Fray Miguel.
A search of Espinosa's house revealed little, as did local inquiries
about the pastry-maker himself. He had practised his trade for
a few months in Nava de Medina before coming to Madrigal some
four months prior to his arrest; and although he had a pastry shop
in Madrigal, someone else made the pastries while Espinosa spent
most of his time at the monastery talking to Doña Ana and Fray
Miguel. It was said that Espinosa's little girl had such fine manners
that she refused to eat without the proper utensils, and the story
of Espinosa's unusual horsemanship is told in greater detail than
that given by Santillán in the *proceso*. After the provincial of the
Order of Saint Augustine forbade Doña Ana and Fray Miguel to

answer Don Rodrigo's questions, an ecclesiastical judge, Juan de Llano y Valdés, was appointed to interrogate the ecclesiastical prisoners.[3]

Chapter iv (fols. 8^v–14^r) deals with the first two confessions of Fray Miguel in which he revealed that Espinosa was really King Sebastian of Portugal and gave detailed reasons in support of the identification. Since this information has been widely used by the literary works, it will be given in full here despite the fact that Fray Miguel later repudiated the confessions. The *proceso* documents do not contain these confessions in full detail, probably because Santillán considered them too ridiculous to send to the king. The items given by Fray Miguel here are some of the stories which were being circulated in Portugal after the Battle of Alcazarquivir.

Fray Miguel testified that he had always believed that Sebastian was not dead because of the many things he had seen and heard. It was said around Lisbon that three men boarded the flagship of the Portuguese fleet the night of the battle. Diogo de Sousa, the commander, then gave the order to sail, saying that one of the men was the king. It that were not true, Sousa would not have left Africa so quickly nor would Cardinal Henrique have let the action go unpunished. When asked why he returned to Portugal without waiting for survivors and more definite news, Sousa put his finger on his lips and replied, "What I did I cannot say, nor could I avoid doing it." The fact that Sebastian had sailed with the fleet was confirmed to Fray Miguel by a soldier who had participated in the battle. That soldier heard the story from another soldier. The day before Fray Miguel was to preach the funeral sermon in Belém, a Portuguese noble told him to be careful of what he said because the king would be present. Two days later the same noble swore to Fray Miguel that Sebastian had attended the service.[4] It was also said that Sebastian had been in the monastery of São Vicente and that Francisca Calva had sent food and clothing for the king to the monastery of Caparica. A friar told Miguel that Sebastian had been in a Carthusian monastery near Badajoz; those monks do not eat meat, and people in the area were shocked to see such a large supply of meat delivered to the monastery. In another monastery, Fray Miguel heard that in a Franciscan monastery a friar said on his death bed that he had heard the king's confession some years after the battle. Fray Miguel had also heard from reliable people that a soldier swore to Cardinal Henrique that he had given Sebastian a drink of water far away from the site of the battle. Another story was that a man had seen a horseman in the Tagus area whom he recognized as Sebastian. When the man fell on his knees, Sebastian put his fingers to his lips, signifying that the man should keep silent, and rode away.

Fray Miguel further testified that he had done special disciplines to find out from God if Sebastian were really alive; and when Espinosa came to Madrigal, Fray Miguel knew that his prayers had been answered. Difficult living conditions and tribulations had changed his appearance, yet Espinosa resembled Sebastian greatly, particularly in the manner of walking and talking. His little girl had the full lower lip and the eyes of the royal family, and Espinosa knew things that only Sebastian could have known. In one conversation Espinosa said, "I have seen myself buried, and I know who mourns me and who does not!"

When asked why Sebastian should live as a humble pastry-maker instead of revealing himself to his people or his uncle, Philip II, Fray Miguel explained that he was so ashamed of giving battle unsuccessfully against the advice of others that he preferred to be considered dead. He had made a vow of penance to wander in the guise of a common man; and when he went to the Pope for release from this vow, absolution was denied because the Pope feared the political disturbances his appearance would cause. Now, after so many years, Sebastian refused to assume his true identity either because he was ashamed of his present station in life or because he feared that Philip would have him executed as an impostor.

Chapter v (fols. 14ʳ–18ᵛ) gives Doña Ana's confessions, following very closely the information contained in the *proceso*. Fray Miguel had told her for some time that her cousin Sebastian was still alive; and when Fray Miguel identified Gabriel de Espinosa as Sebastian, she believed him. She had not told her uncle about Sebastian for fear that he would not believe her or that he would punish Espinosa, and also because she believed Sebastian should not reveal his true identity while Philip II lived. She wanted to spare her uncle's feelings and preferred to arrange things with her cousin Philip after he ascended to the throne.

Doña Ana's account of her first meeting with Espinosa is an interesting item which is not found in the *proceso*. When Fray Miguel first brought Espinosa to the convent grating to meet Doña Ana, Espinosa pretended to be a humble cook, but quite awkwardly as if he were assuming unaccustomed manners. When Doña Ana told him that she wanted to give him some "cargo" (charge) that would be more to his liking than making pastries, Espinosa laughed and replied, "Tengo muy malos hombros para cargas que no naci para ganapan."* After that, he did not hide his identity from her and they had many conversations, during which Espinosa told her many of the same things that Fray Miguel had said previously.

Chapter vi (fols. 19^r–22^r), tells the story of the Portuguese doctor, Manuel Mendes. In the Escorial manuscript his name is Méndez Pacheco, and the Jerez edition calls him Juan Méndez Pacheco. The account given by the *Historia* adds more information to that given by Mendes' confession in the *proceso*. Mendes visited a wounded man at the request of Francisca Calva, and she led him to believe that his patient was the king. When Cardinal Henrique was crowned, an anonymous paper was circulated in the *Córtes* saying that Sebastian was alive and that Mendes had cured him. Mendes was arrested and sent to the galleys, but since there was no proof that he had written the anonymous paper, he was allowed to administer to the galley slaves instead of being chained to an oar. After his release, Fray Miguel coaxed him to leave a good practice in Portugal and come to Madrigal where he could enjoy the patronage of the king's niece. The remainder of the account is identical to that of the *proceso*, even to Doña Ana's angry accusations when Mendes refused to say that Espinosa looked like Sebastian.

Chapter vii (fols. 22^r–25^r) deals with Espinosa's conduct in prison and his first confessions. His testimony under oath concurs with the information given in the *proceso*, but the details of his insinuations (the manuscript calls them "preñeces") and the effective hood-winking of those around him have an aura more of fiction than of fact. At first he insisted that he was a commoner hired by Doña Ana, although he also dropped mysterious hints and assumed grandiose poses that made people about him believe that he must be some important person. Once he was heard to say, "Why ask me who I am? The king and people around him know me well." It was said that once when Santillán started to ask him something secret and special, Espinosa told him in advance what the question would be. Another time Espinosa told Don Rodrigo what the *alcalde* was writing, although the desk was too far away for Espinosa to see the paper. When the little girl's nurse gave birth to a child in prison, Espinosa was asked if the child was his. He replied that if it was, it would have birthmarks in the shape of a sword on one shoulder and a dagger on the other. The baby was examined and found to have the birthmarks specified. An astrologer who came to Medina cast Espinosa's horoscope and announced that he was a great prince.[5]

At last Espinosa confessed that he had pretended to be King Sebastian so that Doña Ana and Fray Miguel would shower him with favors. He was a common man, a humble pastry-maker, who had never known his parents. Santillán had him repeat the confession before witnesses to allay their suspicions and conjectures; however, Espinosa continued to spread confusion by remarking, "You know as little of the truth now as before. Time will tell who I am." He gave the impression that he was protecting others by refusing to tell the truth and continued to assume majestic airs. He did not like to be visited by day and kept his face turned from the light. Once, when a page held the candle too close to him, Espinosa reprimanded the servant with an authority befitting a king. It was said that he even resented the presence of a fly that crossed his room against his wishes.

Chapters viii, ix, and x (fols. 25^r–36^v) reproduce three (of the four) anonymous letters received by Don Rodrigo in Medina del Campo. The first and third letters show only minor copying errors from the originals which do not alter the meaning, and the second letter has been changed slightly to reduce its length. In the Escorial manuscript, two long omissions were made, and the version given by the Jerez edition underwent even more extensive cutting. But more interesting than the deletions are two additions made to the original letter. The anonymous writer remarks that it is interesting to note that although every possible effort is being made to learn Espinosa's identity, the use of torture has been expressly forbidden by Philip. The author of the *Historia* adds the following: "...ni embia quien le conozca, diciendo el presso publicamente que el rey save muy bien quien es, y si no que embie quien le conozca que hartos ay. ..."* In another spot, the letter writer comments on the ridiculous excuse that Sebastian will not reveal himself because of a vow. The original letter reads: "...no se puede dezir que la obligacion del voto le detuvo, y menos la devocion, que por ella sola se privase de un reyno entero."* The Escorial manuscript adds a cutting phrase: "...no se puede dezir que la obligacion del voto le detuvo, y menos la devocion de guardarlo, que de quien andava tras una mugercilla en Valladolid no se puede presumir tanta devocion, que por ella sola se privasse de un reyno entero."*

Chapter xi (fols. 37ʳ-39ʳ) relates the arrest of several people who had nothing to do with the Madrigal case. No names are given, but they can be identified by anyone familiar with the *proceso*. At this time Don Rodrigo noticed that Espinosa's beard was white at the roots where it had grown during his confinement. When the dyed hair was removed, Espinosa appeared to be fifty-five or sixty years old. If Sebastian had lived, he would have been forty.

In Chapter xii (fols. 39ʳ-41ᵛ), Philip II at last consented to the use of torture and Espinosa was moved to Madrigal. There is quite a lengthy narration of his pitiful attempts at bravado during the trip from Medina del Campo to Madrigal.

Chapter xiii (fols. 41ᵛ-47ᵛ) gives the testimony of Fray Miguel under torture. Fray Miguel had planned for years to use the popular belief that Sebastian still lived in order to free Portugal from Spanish domination. Once Portuguese independence was established peacefully by a false Sebastian, the impostor would be killed and Dom António, Prior of Crato, would sit on the throne. In preparation, Fray Miguel kept alive the stories circulating about Sebastian and persuaded Doña Ana that she should marry her cousin when he returned. At last Fray Miguel found a satisfactory impostor in Gabriel de Espinosa, whom he had known as a soldier in Portugal.

The way Fray Miguel prepared Espinosa for assuming his role was clever indeed. Although the details of Espinosa's first encounter with Fray Miguel in Madrigal are not given in the *proceso,* the account here seems quite plausible. Fray Miguel was shrewd enough to known that Espinosa must have complete confidence in the success of the plan and in his ability to convince others that he was Sebastian; consequently, when Fray Miguel talked to Espinosa for the first time, he pretended that he thought Espinosa was Sebastian. Espinosa denied it emphatically at first. Then, when he began to enjoy being treated like a king, he let Fray Miguel persist in his erroneous identification and consented to marry Doña Ana. If he could deceive Fray Miguel, he could deceive anyone. Only then did Fray Miguel reveal the truth to him and started coaching him for the meeting with Doña Ana. The plan was for Espinosa to go to France where Dom António, Antonio Pérez, and Henry IV would support his claim as Sebastian.

In the meantime, Dom António, accompanied by four Portuguese nobles, came to Madrigal at Fray Miguel's request. While Dom António talked to Fray Miguel, three of the nobles called on Espinosa and pretended to acknowledge him as Sebastian. From Madrigal the nobles journeyed to Portugal, spreading the news that they had seen and talked to Sebastian in Madrigal. Some people believed them; others sent representatives to Madrigal to identify the resuscitated king. In the Jerez edition, there is no mention of contact between Portugal and Madrigal after Dom António's visit. Neither the Escorial manuscript nor the Jerez edition indicates that Fray Miguel later retracted this information.

Doña Ana's jewels and the letters which Fray Miguel and Doña Ana wrote to Espinosa calling him "Majesty" were all part of Fray Miguel's plan to give added credence to Espinosa's pose. Fray Miguel had thought out every detail with great care, and Espinosa played his part with gusto. The page who accompanied Espinosa to Valladolid testified that Espinosa sang a ballad about Alcazarquivir on the road, emitting great sighs each time he came to the part about the defeat of the Christian army.

Chapter xiv (fols. 47^v–51^r) reveals more information, not altogether credible, about Espinosa himself. Under torture Espinosa confessed freely, pretending that he never would have revealed anything if Fray Miguel had not confessed first. His story coincided with Fray Miguel's in every detail except for those dealing with Dom António's visit and the plan to put the Prior of Crato on the throne. Espinosa reconfirmed his previous statement that he had never known his parents. He had practised the trades of weaver and pastry-maker in various places, but "mas parecia averse exercitado toda su vida en urdir telas semejantes a la que el y fray Miguel yban urdiendo, que en hazer las de seda o otras materiales."* The rumor was true, he said, that he had left Spain as a young man because of the unfortunate death of an important person. After being a soldier in several countries, he decided that it would be safe to return without being recognized.

The information given by the *ama* indicated that Espinosa's origins were loftier than his confession indicated. She had been with Espinosa for some five years, during which time he occasionally received money from an unknown source. Since he always told her how happy she would be if he could take her to his house in Castile, she assumed that the money came from relatives. The money arrived sporadically, and when they needed more funds, Espinosa had to work at his trade. He had never made pastries with his own hands, however, until they reached Nava de Medina and Madrigal. While in prison, the *ama* gave birth to a handsome boy who looked so much like Espinosa's daughter that there was no doubt but what the *ama* was her mother, as well. Espinosa had claimed that the little girl's mother was a noble lady in Oporto, and there was some conjecture that she might be Doña Ana de Austria. The birth of the second child removed all possibility of doubt.

Although it was now quite clear, even to Doña Ana, that Espinosa was not Sebastian, his real identity was still as much a mystery as before. Espinosa once said that he did not want to name his relatives "para deshonrrarlos que ni se lo devo ni aun se lo deve el que assi me trata."* But, whatever his true origin might have been, Espinosa possessed personal qualities far superior to those of ordinary men, according to the author of the *Historia:* "...son bastantes yndicios de ser persona mas que hordinaria, el buen talle que tenia, gravedad en su persona, y rostro no eran de persona comun, el brio, y el entendimiento y trato publico. Lo mismo el saver tantas lenguas, el ser muy buen hombre de a cavallo, y el aver sido soldado de a cavallo, que esso y el aver hecho muy buenas pruevas de su fuerza y valentia es cosa cierta."*

Chapter xv (fols. 51^r–54^r) begins the sentencing of prisoners. Only Fray Miguel and Espinosa were guilty of active conspiracy, and the others were guilty of participation insofar as they had allowed themselves to be deceived. Doña Ana was the one most wronged by the imposture, yet her sentence was a severe one. The manuscript gives an accurate copy of the sentences of Doña Ana and her two friends, Doña Luisa Grado and Doña María Nieto.

The remainder of the chapter is devoted to a rather lengthy account of how a courier was apprehended, carrying a package of letters for Doña Ana. The author did not know what the letters contained but they apparently appealed to his love for the mysterious; consequently, the incident was put into the *Historia.* The letters were no doubt those sent by the prisoner of Évora (see above, Ch. iv, note 11).

Chapter xvi (fols. 54^r–59^r) deals primarily with Espinosa's delaying maneuvers after his sentence was decided and the great efforts made by a Jesuit priest to prepare him for death. Espinosa insisted that there had been no baseness in his crime to warrant hanging. He wished to appeal his sentence; and when he was assured that Philip II himself had already approved the manner of his death, he said that he would appeal it to the throne of God. This rebellious attitude continued, and the priest struggled with the recalcitrant prisoner for three days. On Monday, the day before the execution, Espinosa's spiritual staff was augmented by two discalced friars; but his assumed role had possessed him so completely that he often raved like an insane man, making veiled references to his family and complaining because the king had sent no one to identify him. The three priests stayed with him all night, fighting to free his soul from the devil's grip.

Chapter xvii (fols. 59^r-63^v) relates Espinosa's last hours and his death in great detail. The author, who came from Medina del Campo with a Jesuit priest to witness the execution, gives a vivid description of Espinosa on the morning of his death:

Yo confieso que llevava gran lastima y compassion por las cossas que havia oydo, y que se me doblo en viendole porque le hable en cuerpo con un gregesco y ropilla de terciopelo muy pulida y una media de aguja muy estirada y el con un semblante y tan buena conversacion como si nada hubiera passado ni huviera de passar por el, tanto que estando a la sazon con los guardas dude que era el presso, y si no me dijeran nada antes juzgara que era qualquiera de los circunstantes que el.*

Espinosa's mood was belligerent and his mien haughty. He was obviously not ready to accept death contritely, so the Jesuits asked for Santillán's help. The *alcalde* had the *serón* brought into the street and the rope placed around the prisoner's neck as if he were to be led out for immediate execution. This seemed to restore Espinosa's sense of reality, and he spent the remaining time in confession.

The manuscript's account of Espinosa's execution—his reaction when the traveler entered, his remarks about the wording of the *pregón,* and his attitude on the gallows—follows very closely the accounts given by Fuensalida and Santillán in the *proceso.* There is some small variation in the details concerning who said what, but the essence of the remarks is identical.

Chapter xviii (fols. 63^v-68^r) gives the execution of Fray Miguel in Madrid quite accurately despite the fact that the author, by his own admission, was not there. He speaks of the confrontation with the prisoners from Portugal, but he was unaware that Fray Miguel made a last retraction as a result. Fray Miguel heard his sentence read in the Church of San Martín on October 16. The Archbishop of Oristán then read the *auto* of degradation, and Fray Miguel was handed over to the civil authorities. Three days later he was taken to the gallows, accompanied by four priests. As he began to mount the steps, he said in a low, clear voice that he deserved death although he was not guilty of the major crimes for which he was condemned. He had not conspired against Philip II, acting as he did because he had really believed that Espinosa was Sebastian. He had not written to Dom António nor had he heard from him. If he confessed otherwise, it was because of fear of torture. As Fray Miguel mounted the steps, the notary approached and asked him some questions that Fray Miguel answered with "animo y brio" (spirit and verve) although the conversation was inaudible even to those standing near. Fray Miguel gripped a crucifix firmly as the hangman adjusted the rope, and he died quickly.

The moral lesson pointed out by the author is to beware of the devil's influence which leads to such madness. Fray Miguel and Espinosa believed, even after they were imprisoned, that they could persuade people to accept their deception. Espinosa played his role on the gallows as if he had, in reality, become the one he pretended to be. He had risen so high in his imagination that he could not find the way down to reality.

The Jerez edition has added another paragraph as an item of interest. Once when Fray Miguel was dining with the archbishop in Burgos, a great mathematician and astrologer, who was sitting at the same table, stared at Fray Miguel in a disturbed fashion. Alone with the archbishop later, the astrologer complained, "I'm ready to burn my books. This upsets me!" When asked why he was distressed, he explained that according to all indications of his science, Fray Miguel would die by hanging. The archbishop laughed.

This, then, was the "historical" account of the "Pastelero de Madrigal" which stirred the imaginations of later writers. Basically the writer of the *Historia* presented a factual account. He makes it quite clear that Espinosa was not Sebastian of Portugal but an adventurer who served as a tool for Fray Miguel's attempt to place the crown of Portugal on the head of Dom António. The fact that Espinosa's true identity was never established attracted the author, however, and he emphasized the qualities in Espinosa which heightened the aura of mystery surrounding his person. The *proceso* documents show that Espinosa was a common rogue with a flair for the dramatic. He played his role when he had a receptive audience; but when those around him were not easily hoodwinked, as in the case of Don Rodrigo, Espinosa was sullen, depressed, and afraid. At his execution Espinosa had a large audience and gave his last performance with great competence, but most of the anecdotes related in the *Historia* about his remarkable talents seem to be based more on rumor than on fact. Because of their extravagant nature, these details are the ones utilized by writers who were attracted by the figure of the bizarre *pastelero*. Let us review them briefly: Espinosa's apparent disregard of money and lack of interest in his pastry shop; his little girl's meticulous eating habits; his departure from Spain because of killing an important person; the money he received from unknown sources; his strange powers of penetration and imperious manner; the birthmarks on the *ama's* second baby; Espinosa's dyed hair and beard; his singing the ballad about Alcazarquivir; and the visit of the Portuguese nobles. From Fray Miguel there are detailed reasons why he believed Sebastian was still alive and why he believed Espinosa was Sebastian, as well as Fray Miguel's mysterious conversation with the notary at his execution.

The future roles of other characters are indicated by the *Historia*. Because it was written and published before the death of Philip II, the author had no choice but to minimize the participation of Doña Ana de Austria, the king's harsh treatment of his niece, and the widespread belief that she was the little girl's mother. This reduces the importance of her position in the conspiracy, and Doña Ana becomes a pitiful but colorless creature who fades into the background as Espinosa acquires more strength and complexity. Juan de Llano also gradually disappears while Don Rodrigo, because of his contact with Espinosa, moves into the position of persecutor as well as prosecutor.

The cast is complete. The dramatic situations and intrigue are ready-made, waiting for the first author to give the story artistic form.

VI

THE
PASTELERO IN
SPANISH
LITERATURE

*T*he transforming process by which a historical personage moves into literature and acquires the characteristics and stature of a legendary figure is, of necessity, a gradual one. In the case of Gabriel de Espinosa, the metamorphosis took two and a half centuries. The historical account of the political conspiracy and the first appearance of the *pastelero* in literature could not depart violently from the factual relation of a bizarre plot to pass a Spanish pastry-maker off as the King of Portugal. With the passage of time, however, greater liberties could be, and were taken until Espinosa and King Sebastian were fused into a single legendary figure in the minds of the Spanish reading public. The literary works dealing with the incident of the *pastelero* are not of great artistic merit but their popularity attests to the unfailing appeal of a clever impersonation and a daring conspiracy that could have changed the course of national history. Although the historical role of the real Gabriel de Espinosa would have been impossible without the Portuguese search for a national messiah and the accompanying insistence that Sebastian still lived, the literary metamorphosis of the *pastelero* is not directly related to the development of the Sebastianist cult in Portugal during or after the restoration of Portuguese independence in 1640. Portuguese Sebastianism may have heightened the Spanish authors' interest in the conspiracy, but the *pastelero* has not taken on the religious, messianic qualities of the Portuguese *Encoberto,* nor has he aroused great interest in Portuguese writers beyond his historical existence as one of the four false Dom Sebastians. The stream of events which began with the death of Sebastian and the union of Spain and Portugal divided in the seventeenth century and became two distinct currents, each held by the confines of its national language: the Portuguese waited for the return of Sebastian, *O Encoberto,* the national messiah, while the Spanish remolded their *pastelero* into the tragic figure of a martyred monarch.

The first literary interpretation of the Madrigal event was a *comedia* bearing the title *El Pastelero de Madrigal.* It was published anonymously in three *suelta* editions in the mid-eighteenth century —Madrid, [s. a.]; [Madrid], 1746; and Valencia, 1765—but its structure, typical of the *comedia* of the *Siglo de Oro,* indicates that it was written earlier. The writer of the article, "Madrigal, Pastelero de," in the *Enciclopedia universal ilustrada europeo-americana* (Barcelona, 1907—), gives the date of composition as 1706 and names José de Cañizares as the author. More frequently, however, the work is attributed to Jerónimo de Cuéllar who died sometime after 1665.[1] There is little variation in the texts of the three editions except for spelling changes and stage directions. The Madrid edition without date is more like the Valencia edition of 1765 than the Madrid edition of 1746 and appears to have been printed in the interval between the other two. The Madrid edition of 1746 omits "una niña" completely from the list of characters and gives "Laura" who appears in the text as "Clara." These errors are corrected in the two later editions. Quotations appearing here will be from the edition of Valencia, 1765.

The *Pastelero de Madrigal* is a *comedia* in three acts, based on the *Historia de Gabriel de Espinosa.* A few characters and a subplot of amorous intrigue were added to make the work conform to the Golden Age *comedia* pattern, but they do not detract from the central theme of Espinosa's impersonation. Under the tutelege of Fray Miguel dos Santos, who is disguised as a student, Gabriel de Espinosa hopes to convince Doña Ana de Austria and a group of

Portuguese nobles that he is King Sebastian of Portugal. Dressed in regal splendor, he successfully receives three Portuguese nobles who have traveled to Madrigal to verify his identity. The nobles, easily deceived by Espinosa's royal appearance and clever lies, accept him joyfully as their monarch. Two return to Portugal to spread the news that Sebastian is really not dead and the third, Don Sancho, stays in Madrigal to aid Espinosa in dispatching and receiving mail. Espinosa is equally convincing in his interview with Doña Ana de Austria and the conspiracy seems to be on the verge of success when Don Rodrigo de Santillana comes to Madrigal, ostensibly to arrange for his marriage to Leonor, Don Sancho's daughter, but also for the purpose of discharging some secret official obligation in the service of the king. The nature of Don Rodrigo's mysterious assignment is revealed at the end of Act II, when he surprises Espinosa and Miguel again entertaining the visiting Portuguese nobles and takes them all to jail. Don Rodrigo's interrogation of Doña Ana, Fray Miguel, the Portuguese nobles, and Espinosa's servants reveals that all believe the pastry-maker to be King Sebastian of Portugal. Although the *alcalde* himself is loath to accredit their statements, Gabriel's equivocal answers, majestic bearing, and commanding personality finally force the *alcalde* to doubt his own judgment. Don Rodrigo's dilemma is conveniently resolved, however, by a ghost who appears to Miguel and orders him, in God's name, to confess the deceit. The right to rule comes from God alone and God will not permit a common trickster (*embustero*) to sit on the throne of Portugal. After Fray Miguel's confession, Espinosa has little choice but to tell the sordid story of his own life. He was found on the church steps in Toledo and reared by a friar. After a disagreement with the friar, he started on a long series of trades—weaver, soldier, *pregonero*, sacristan, and pastry-maker—but his real profession was that of *embustero:*

> Si soy galante y valiente,
> bien lo publican las muestras;
> mas qué importa, si malogro
> estas virtudes excelsas

con ser tan grande embustero?
que si hubiese competencia
de enredadores, ganara
yo la Cátedra primera.

Although in the next breath Espinosa hints that his confession was false, Don Rodrigo's doubts are dispelled and he brings the *proceso* to a speedy close. Gabriel is executed, continuing his *embustes* to the steps of the gallows where he calls out Don Rodrigo's name in a last vain challenge. Sentence is swiftly passed on the other participants of the political conspiracy and all remaining characters assemble for a standard *comedia* ending of multiple betrothals.

The subplot of amorous intrigue, appearing principally in the first two acts, serves a three-fold purpose: it adds depth and emphasis to Espinosa's ability to maintain several identities and dominate those around him, heightening dramatic suspense; it reveals an ignoble side of Espinosa's character that holds in check the audience's excessive sympathy for him as a person; and it permits the intrusion of situations so beloved to the audiences of the *comedia de capa y espada*—masked men hidden and discovered in a lady's house, mistaken identities, two unexpected male visitors hidden in the same room, the wronged maid confronting her lover, arranged marriage conflicting with the desires of the participants, etc. The central figure of these amorous complications is Leonor, daughter of Don Sancho, who is being courted simultaneously by Gabriel de Espinosa, Don Rodrigo de Santillana, and Don Fadrigue. Leonor rejects Don Fadrigue and is cool to the marriage with Don Rodrigo which her father hopes to arrange, favoring the attentions of Espinosa whom she believes to be a Portuguese noble, Don Juan de Silva. Espinosa's relations with the household of Don Sancho are further complicated by the presence of Leonor's servant, Clara, who is, in reality, Espinosa's former paramour and the mother of Espinosa's small daughter. Clara has followed Espinosa to Madrigal in the hope that he will fulfil his promise to marry her.

One of the most popular sources of inspiration for the Golden Age theater was Spanish history. In this case, the author of the *comedia* has drawn heavily on the *Historia de Gabriel de Espinosa* for both plot and characters. The political intrigue, in particular, follows the *Historia* in almost every detail, one notable exception being the circumstances of Gabriel's arrest. It is interesting to note the particular items of the historical narrative—other than the general structure of the conspiracy—which were utilized by the dramatic piece. For example, the presence of the three Portuguese nobles is based on the *Historia* account of Dom António's visit to Madrigal and the nobles who called upon Espinosa; however, their roles have been enlarged in the *comedia* to give more emphasis to Gabriel's ability to play the part of a king. The details of Espinosa's first meeting with Doña Ana and the manner in which she forced him to accept the jewels are identical to the account of the *Historia*. Gabriel's fit of rage when he hears the ballad about Alcazarquivir has a double source: his singing of the ballad en route to Valladolid and his majestic outbursts in prison. In Act III, the scene in which Espinosa is questioned by Santillana is an outgrowth of the *Historia's* relation of Gabriel's extra-sensory powers and the manner in which he treated the jailers. The confessions of both Gabriel and Fray Miguel, Espinosa's hint that his confession was not true, the servants' testimony about Gabriel's generosity and income of unknown source, and Gabriel's conduct on the scaffold are all taken from the *Historia.*[2]

The central figure of Gabriel de Espinosa is essentially that of the *Historia*. The *comedia* has utilized the *Historia's* presentation of a remarkable man whose commanding airs and great experience in *embustes* mystified all those around him. In the *Historia,* however, one sees a less majestic side of Espinosa, and at times he is a pitiful creature who is led to a horrible death by his own vanity and Fray Miguel's trickery. This is not true of Gabriel of the *comedia*. Even Don Rodrigo, the poised and duty-bound officer of the law, is not immune to Gabriel's overwhelming personality. Gabriel never steps out of character. Even when confessing that he was a foundling abandoned at the church door in Toledo, he seems motivated more by rage at Fray Miguel's weakness than by fear of punishment. He is the master of deceits and the able manner in which he sustains three different identities throughout the first two acts of the *comedia* makes one believe that he would have been successful in the greatest impersonation of all, the resuscitated Sebastian, if it had not been for divine intervention. The characterization of Gabriel is excellent throughout the play, but it is particularly effective in the closing scene of Act II when Don Rodrigo makes the arrests and in the scene laid in Gabriel's cell when he is being questioned. Although the denouement of the play is weak, the character of Gabriel does not suffer.

As the role of Gabriel grows in complexity, the characterizations of the other principal figures in the political intrigue fade into the background. Doña Ana does not appear on stage and is referred to only as a rather colorless and simple-minded creature, easily controlled by Miguel and Gabriel. Although Miguel was the originator of the political scheme, his character in the *comedia* loses stature. In his confession he identifies himself as Dom António's former confessor, yet in his disguise as a student he lacks dignity and respect. His conduct with Gabriel is quite servile, and his sneering asides about placing Dom António on the throne have a villainous air. Even the Portuguese nobles give him no attention, and his abject terror after the appearance of the ghost (his conscience, perhaps) diminishes the dramatic force of his confession.

The character of Gabriel's little girl, *la niña,* is used in the *comedia* to give added strength to his impersonation. As in the *Historia,* she looks like the royal family of Portugal and demands luxuries unheard-of in the daughter of a humble *pastelero.* The character of her mother, Clara, is based on the *ama* of the *Historia.*[3] In the *comedia,* however, she has taken on qualities more in keeping with the *capa y espada* tradition. She is the aggrieved woman who pursues her lover with the demand that he marry her, thereby restoring her honor. Adding to the amorous intrigue is her position as maid in the house of Leonor, current object of Gabriel's attentions.

In general, the author of the *comedia* has joined together smoothly the political conspiracy and the *comedia* elements of amorous intrigue. The development of both themes is continued effectively until the appearance of the ghost in the middle of Act III, at which time the dramatic structure collapses. The author cannot find a satisfactory way to end the play. The reason given for the failure of the conspiracy seems to be a vague defense of the divine right of kings, but even this thesis is not clearly presented. It would have been much more effective to have Miguel confess when torture was applied; however, this would have left his testimony open to doubt as to its validity, and the audience would, perhaps, have felt too much sympathy for the *pastelero*. The author was faced with a dual problem: that of making it quite clear to the audience that Gabriel was an impostor, and that of maintaining the dramatic strength of his character. The failure to find a satisfactory solution has damaged the dramatic impact of the play as a whole. The concluding scenes do not live up to expectations produced by the first two and one-half acts.

In spite of a weak ending, the *comedia* contains an artistic unity centered in the person of Gabriel de Espinosa, a powerful and dramatic figure who dominates the entire play. The metamorphosis of the *pastelero* has begun. The poor devil of the *proceso,* a hapless pawn dragged to his death by Fray Miguel's desperate struggle for the political independence of Portugal, has developed into a complex and commanding figure, the pivotal point of all action and the key to all intrigue.

During the eighteenth century many Golden Age *comedias* were rewritten to make them conform to the rigid rules of neo-classical style, chiefly the unities of time, place, and action. *El Pastelero de Madrigal* also has its *refundición,* "El Pastelero de Madrigal, comedia en 5 actos," an anonymous manuscript in the theatrical collection of Arturo Sedó in Barcelona. It has not been published, and since it does not improve in any respect on the *comedia,* it is unlikely that it will be. This *refundición* is not a rewriting or a new interpretation but a re-shuffling of the *comedia.* The writer has rearranged the scenes of the *comedia* into five acts, reducing the amount of amorous intrigue and adding perhaps a total of sixty original lines. The original scenes have been subject to a certain amount of cutting to make the new sequence cohesive; but, by and large, one can match the scenes from the *refundición* with those of the *comedia* line for line.

In the *comedia* the time element is ill-defined. There are no divisions into scenes or specific references to the passage of time that might help determine what span of time is covered by the action, but it is long enough to allow the Portuguese nobles to go to Portugal and return. In the last act, this vacuity is particularly disturbing when Gabriel seems to be hanged immediately after his confession. The time span of the *refundición* is much shorter. Although there is no specific duration of time stated, the action appears to begin on one day, move through that night, and terminate on the following day with Gabriel's confession. His execution does not take place in the play.

The action, as well, is more compact in the *refundición*. The amorous intrigue which built up the importance of minor characters in the *comedia* has been reduced, and the two big scenes in the *comedia* with the Portuguese nobles has been fused into one in the *refundición*. Through Act IV the structure of the *refundición* may be considered an improvement over that of the *comedia* by those who object to the choppy scenes and diffuse action of the latter type, but the last act of the *refundición* is even weaker than the ending of the *comedia*. The motive for Miguel's confession is not given at all and the fact that none of the prisoners' sentence is settled gives the impression that the last scene was omitted. The *comedia* tied up loose ends hastily and haphazardly, but the *refundición* leaves them dangling.

In short, the *refundición* does not eliminate the defects of the *comedia,* principally that of a weak ending, nor does it preserve the qualities which make the *comedia* entertaining. The strength of the *comedia* lies in the dashing, bizarre figure of Gabriel, but the *refundición* has weakened that character by reducing him to the level of an ambitious opportunist, lacking dramatic depth.

The Romantic Movement in Spain brought about a revival of

interest in national history and legends which had also flourished
as inspiration for literary works during the Golden Age. The tragic
figure of the headstrong young king, Sebastian of Portugal, possessed
all the qualities necessary for a hero of the romantic period:
courage, religious fervor, desire for personal glory, and a tragic
death which brought economic ruin and political oppression to his
country. In nineteenth-century Portugal, *sebastianistas* still composed
new *trovas* and waited for the return of the *Encoberto.* Portuguese
interest in Sebastian was sustained by the desire for national prosperity and political power, ambitions that were not supported by
their Castilian neighbors; however, Spain had her own link with
Sebastian through the unique pastry-maker, executed in Madrigal
by Philip II. Earlier Spanish writers, while emphasizing the mystery
surrounding the person of Gabriel de Espinosa, presented him as an
impostor who was discovered and rightfully punished. In the
nineteenth century Spain was no longer sensitive about the re-
establishment of Portuguese independence some two hundred years
before, nor was it considered blasphemous to criticize the policies
or the person of Philip II. The romantic writer, then, was at liberty
to give the event any interpretation he chose.

This opportunity was first seized by Patricio de la Escosura[4]
who realized that the tragic quality of Sebastian's fate would be
increased if he were forced to witness the disastrous effects of his
rashness. By presenting Gabriel de Espinosa as the real Sebastian,
Escosura makes the unfortunate monarch drink the last dregs of
a very bitter cup. Deprived of a hero's death on the battlefield,
Sebastian becomes a fugitive, persecuted by the agents of Philip II.
After years of hiding and scheming, the revolt against Spanish
domination is organized and Sebastian is ready to shed his igno-
minious disguise as a commoner. On the eve of his departure
from Valladolid to Portugal, he is arrested and executed as an impostor. This is a fate worthy of a monarch whose destiny is misfortune.

Escosura's novel, *Ni rey ni roque,* published in 1835 when its
author was twenty-eight years old, uses as its historical source the

Jerez edition of the *Historia de Gabriel de Espinosa*. Escosura pretends, however, that the author of the *Historia* was afraid to tell the entire truth because Philip II still lived when his account appeared. The novel is presented as a "true" relation of the Sebastian-Espinosa story, written by a follower of King Sebastian and preserved by Sebastian's descendants whom Escosura discovered in Andalusia.

Escosura has used the *Historia* account of the political conspiracy, but he reveals it slowly to the reader through the experiences of a young Castilian noble, Don Juan de Vargas, who becomes entangled in the *pastelero's* affair by falling in love with Inés, later identified as the sister-in-law of Gabriel de Espinosa. Fray Miguel dos Santos and Gabriel, knowing that Don Juan's noble name and military experience will be valuable contributions to their cause, finally take him into their confidence and reveal the startling fact that Gabriel de Espinosa is, in reality, Sebastian of Portugal. After the Battle of Alcazarquivir, Sebastian secretly returned to Portugal with the fleet, preferring to be considered dead after the humiliating defeat. Cardinal Henrique's persecution of Sebastian's friends drove him out of Portugal and subsequent persecutions by agents of Philip II forced him to wander around Europe for eight years, accompanied by a small group of faithful followers. Now eager to reclaim his throne, Sebastian returned to Portugal, using as his headquarters a remote estate belonging to Francisca de Alba (Francisca Calva in the *Historia* and the *proceso*), where her young orphaned kinswomen, Clara and Inés Contiño, lived. Several years later Sebastian and Clara were married, and the king and his followers traveled to Italy where Sebastian hoped to obtain papal release from his vow of penance. Fearful of political disturbances and the displeasure of Spain, the Pope refused absolution. Sebastian was recognized and imprisoned by Spanish authorities in Naples, but his friends effected his escape and the group fled to France where Clara contracted tuberculosis and died, leaving her small daughter in the care of her sister, Inés. A year later they moved to Madrigal, where Sebastian established a pastry shop under the assumed name of Gabriel de Espinosa. Fray Miguel dos Santos won the support of

Doña Ana de Austria and Portuguese nobles visited them frequently. Don Juan de Vargas willingly joins the conspiracy to restore Sebastian's crown in order to win Inés' hand. As plans for the uprising near completion, Sebastian, continuing his role as Espinosa, moves into Valladolid where the larger gatherings of armed men can be more easily concealed. Jewels given him by Doña Ana attract attention, causing his arrest, and the intercepted mail reveals the complicity of Fray Miguel and Doña Ana. Gabriel refuses to reveal his true identity or to name accomplices, thereby protecting the many people, both Spanish and Portuguese, who have pledged their support. Under torture Sebastian and Fray Miguel confess to anything the investigating officers want to hear and are condemned to die for treason. After their death Don Juan retires to an estate in Andalusia with Inés and Clarita, Sebastian's daughter. It is from their descendants that Escosura learns the "true" account of King Sebastian's death.

The conception of Gabriel de Espinosa as King Sebastian brings new dignity to the characters of Gabriel, Fray Miguel, and Doña Ana. Escosura's Gabriel is a regal figure who demands the same unquestioning obedience now that he did almost twenty years before on the plains of Alcazarquivir, and his proud determination again ends in tragedy. This time, however, he is strong enough to face the consequences of his actions: "...murio de la muerte de los malhechores, con el mismo aliento que un mártir" (IV, 6).* Fray Miguel is a just man and exemplary priest who deserves the trust of Doña Ana and the respect of the people of Madrigal. His is no longer a merciless scheme to place a pretender on the throne of Portugal by sacrificing a nun's confidence and an adventurer's life, but a just and noble cause for which he forfeits his life with willing resignation. Doña Ana is still the innocent victim, not of Fray Miguel's deceit this time, but of man's political institutions and the policies of Philip II: "La misma política estrecha, mezquina y tiránica que jamas concedió al vencedor de Lepanto las prerogativas de infante de España...esa misma hizo monja á doña Ana" (II,

* Translations of starred passages may be found in Appendix B.

5).* Although she accepted her religious profession in obedience to the desires of her royal uncle, Doña Ana yearned to be a wife and mother. The appearance of Sebastian meant a chance for her liberty and for happiness, but her dreams ended in disgrace and confinement. Philip II is the villain of Escosura's work: "Cobarde, como su padre valiente; cruel, como aquel generoso; y fanático, como religioso era Carlos, ningún crimen arredraba á Felipe cuando se trataba de su seguridad, de su venganza, ó de los mal entendidos intereses de su religión" (II, 5).* Escosura uses Philip's persecution of Sebastian's friends after the union of Spain and Portugal as a typical example of his tyranny and hypocrisy. Not only does Philip order the assassination of his own son, Don Carlos, and that of his nephew, Sebastian, but he even guards the secret of the latter crime by having the *alcalde* in charge of the *proceso* imprisoned and garroted.

Escosura's portrayal of the *alcalde,* Don Rodrigo Santillana, presents an interesting side light on sixteenth-century Spain as seen through nineteenth-century eyes. He is an ambitious young officer of the law who cultivates the friendship of Don Juan de Vargas to gain the good will of an influential family and who performs his duties for the king with eager thoroughness. Philip, however, like most tyrants, did not trust his agents, "juzgando al género humano por su corazón" (IV, 3).* In an audience with the king before Gabriel's betrayal and arrest, Santillana's hopes for royal appreciation are crushed by Philip's deliberate, cruel scorn for his efficiency. The frightened *alcalde* is so upset that he goes to bed with a fever. The court physicians make an erroneous diagnosis, forbidding him to drink water; and if a servant had not taken pity on the suffering man and given him all the water he craved, the fever would have ended his life. Don Rodrigo came to Madrid with great expectations of royal favor, but he returns to Valldolid thankful that he is alive. The next time that he goes to Madrid to report to Philip II, he is not so fortunate.

The romantic spirit of personal independence is present throughout *Ni rey ni roque*. As well as censuring the tyranny of political institutions in sixteenth-century Spain, Escosura makes a bitter attack on the Inquisition and the suffocating power it exercised over the entire country. A defense of religious tolerance is presented through the character of Gabriel de Espinosa, who accepts the support of Spanish Protestants and gives them, in return, a written guarantee of religious freedom in Portugal,[5] and through Don Juan de Vargas who overcomes his reluctance to associate with heretics and consents to be the leader of the Protestant group.

It is unfortunate that the popularity of *Ni rey ni roque* has been eclipsed by that of *El Pastelero de Madrigal* by Manuel Fernández y González. In the development of plot, presentation of characters, and quality of literary composition, *Ni rey ni roque* is far superior to *El Pastelero de Madrigal,* yet the former was reprinted only in 1841 and 1963 while the latter, first published in 1862, is still being reprinted in Spain and Spanish America with astounding frequency.[6] One cannot say that the poor taste of the reading public is entirely to blame. Tastes in literary style change, and any work which follows the extremes of a literary vogue runs the risk of soon becoming dated. Escosura addresses himself to the reader in a chatty tone, often digressing to compare the dress, manners, and customs of sixteenth-century Spain with those of his own day, and his lengthy tirades on political and religious freedom impede plot development. The imprint of the Romantic Movement is also evident in Escosura's descriptions of nature (idyllic or ominous) and treatment of characters who are not directly inspired by the historical account of the *Historia de Gabriel de Espinosa.* Clara, Gabriel's wife and the mother of the little girl, is a delicate, blond beauty who spends her short life exuding sweet sadness. Her sister, Inés, is darker in complexion and more robust physically, but she is distressed by recurring premonitions of disaster; and after Gabriel's death and her subsequent marriage to Don Juan, she continues to live under the pall of unhappy memories. The motivating force for all of Don Juan's actions is his deep love for Inés which brings him to risk name, fortune, and life to serve a foreign king.

Although *El Pastelero de Madrigal* is not, in like manner, dated by the excesses and irrelevances of the early romantic novel, Fernández y González has sacrificed everything else to action, and his Gabriel de Espinosa goes through six hundred pages of fantastic, action-packed adventures. In Africa, Venice, and Spain, his path crosses with that of dozens of exotic characters whose mysterious and tragic backgrounds fill an equal number of chapters and whose lives, on the whole, have no direct bearing on Espinosa's dual identity as King Sebastian of Portugal and adventurer-soldier Gabriel de Espinosa.

Chronoligically, *El Pastelero de Madrigal* follows José Zorrilla's play, *Traidor, inconfeso y mártir,* which was first presented in 1849; but since the work of Fernández y González offers no new interpretation of the character of Gabriel de Espinosa, no step forward in the metamorphosis from pastry cook to king, strict observance of chronology is unimportant here. If we were to be influenced only by artistic merit of the work or its contribution to the multi-sided picture of the *pastelero* in literature, the novel of Fernández y González would warrant no more attention than a brief listing with other minor works on the subject.[7] But the immense popularity of *El Pastelero de Madrigal,* even through the present day, forces a brief commentary here, albeit negative in tone.

Fernández y González has drawn from a variety of sources for the construction of a novelistic plot that defies brief summarization. The rescue of Sebastian (or Gabriel) by a Moorish family after the Battle of Alcazarquivir appears in several Spanish literary works about Sebastian;[8] José Zorrilla's play, *Traidor, inconfeso y mártir,* supplies the germs for Gabriel's activities as a pirate, his association with the Venetian state, and the daughter of Don Rodrigo de Santillana; and the account of Gabriel's arrest and execution is taken from the *Historia de Gabriel de Espinosa* which is quoted directly on several occasions. Upon this eclectic framework, Fernández y González has released a cataract of swirling events that follow each other in a seemingly endless procession. The plot is constructed in a careless, slipshod way, filled with contradictory statements about the age, physical appearance, or relationships of the myriad characters and with historical inaccuracies. Descriptions are unimaginative, generally consisting of a listing of well-worn, oft-repeated adjectives. The characters lack motivation and their reactions arouse little sympathy in the reader. Gabriel, the central figure, demonstrates well the superficial, hasty manner in which the characters are delineated. His conduct with Mirian (his wife) and Aben Shariar (his only true friend), to whom he owes so much, indicates a petty, inappreciative spirit, and his constant reminders that he will always be a mystery to them leave little to the reader's imagination. He arouses no sympathy or understanding in the reader who never knows—and after six hundred pages no longer cares—whether he is really Gabriel or Sebastian. The righteous tone with which he tells the *alcalde* Don Rodrigo that he is not Sebastian and never pretended to be is in direct contradiction to his previous behavior; consequently, the divine wrath which falls on Don Rodrigo for executing him seems unjust, and the vision experienced by the dying *alcalde* in which he sees Gabriel and Mirian, wearing martyrs' crowns and smiling forgivingly at him from eternity, is ludicrous.

The complete artistic fusion of King Sebastian with Gabriel de Espinosa was achieved by José Zorrilla in the drama, *Traidor, inconfeso y mártir,* first presented in 1849. Zorrilla had long been attracted by the story of the bizarre pastry-maker, but Escosura's novel, *Ni rey ni roque,* was an obstacle that blocked the creative development of Zorrilla's concept of the character of Gabriel.[9] The original pastry-maker masqueraded as the king, and Escosura's Sebastian posed as Gabriel. Zorrilla was satisfied with neither. At last he succeeded in fusing the persons of the king and pastry-maker into a single figure, thus creating a new, artistic character with highly dramatic possibilities. Escosura's Sebastian always remains a personage, rather than a person. He is viewed from a respectful distance by the reader who is never permitted to penetrate the regal reserve or witness the conflicts and emotions that struggle for control in the human heart. Zorrilla's Gabriel can be labeled neither pastry cook nor king, or he may be ascribed either title, indifferently. It is impossible to divide this Gabriel into two persons or two roles. Zorrilla presents a man, an unusual man, it is true, but one who maintains his spiritual independence regardless of name or title. His is a complex, yet integral personality. He has the power to attract and dominate other humans, extract from them love and obedience or drive them to anger and violence; yet he stands aloof from others, even those who are willing to risk their lives to aid him. This very reserve comes from a warm, human desire to protect others, to avoid dragging them with him toward the unhappy fate that Gabriel knows he cannot avoid. Although Zorrilla states that he studied the *proceso* documents, he has utilized the historical event only as a springboard for his imagination. The name of the *alcalde*, Don Rodrigo de Santillana, and the details contained in Gabriel's sentence (including the names of Fray Miguel dos Santos and Doña Ana de Austria) are based on history, but the rest is an artistic creation of fantasy, built around the powerful figure of Gabriel.

José Zorrilla, re-creator of Spanish legends, is Spain's most beloved dramatist of the nineteenth century. With Spanish history of the Middle Ages as the principal inspiration of his dramatic plots and the *comedia* of the Golden Age as a model, Zorrilla became the dominating figure of Spanish romantic drama. He captured the essence of the *comedia* and gave it modern expression, endowing its personages, not necessarily with the emotions they must have had, but with those that the audience wanted them to have. The valor, nobility, and daring of past centuries were portrayed with passion and grandeur in the "leyendas escenificadas"[10] which were Zorrilla's dramas. Zorrilla took pride in his role as reviver of a patriotic drama, calling himself "el poeta del tiempo viejo."[11]

In his autobiographical *Recuerdos del tiempo viejo*, Zorrilla devotes an entire chapter to reminiscences about the writing and production of *Traidor, inconfeso y mártir*. It was his last work written for the stage and it was his favorite, the only one that gave him artistic satisfaction. In his own words: "Estudié su historia y su tradición, dormí y soñé con la accion y sus personajes, y cuando la ví clara en mi imaginación comencé á tenderla sobre el papel: y aquella es mi única obra dramática pensada, coordinada y *hecha*, segun las reglas del arte: sus dos primeros actos están confeccionados maestramente, y tengo para mí que por ellos tengo derecho á que mi nombre figure entre los de los dramáticos de mi siglo" (pp. 205-6).*

Zorrilla's pride in *Traidor, inconfeso y mártir*, particularly the first two acts, is justified. The plot is constructed with care and the action progresses steadily through the natural-sounding dialogue without a superfluous word. All interest is focused on the character of Gabriel, mysterious and dramatic, but drawn with a restraint that adds dignity and depth. Gabriel does not appear on the stage until late in the first act although he has been the principal topic of conversation from the opening scene. The interest and suspense built up by his late appearance are sustained, and even intensified, by his first conversation with Don César. Gabriel has been announced as a strange man whose remarkable qualities intimate that he is more than his humble name and profession indicate. He is a solitary person who rejects friendship and flees from confidences. When Gabriel finally does appear in the flesh, he is no disappointment. His cool dignity in repulsing Don César's advances simultaneously attracts and enrages the young man, and the skilful way in which he avoids entanglement at the same time that he increases the aura of mystery surrounding his person is a superb demonstration of Zorrilla's ability to write dialogue in poetry.

For the benefit of those who do not know *Traidor, inconfeso y mártir,* let us follow the unfolding of Zorrilla's powerful characterization of Gabriel through the play, act by act. Perhaps such a summary, although somewhat pedestrian, will communicate an idea of the skill with which Zorrilla has constructed this dramatic piece and of the emotional force of its presentation.

The first act opens as three men in succession come to an innkeeper in Valladolid, giving him money to care for the comforts of three travelers—Aurora, her father, and a servant—who will arrive later. The first man is the Marquis of Tavira, a Portuguese noble; the second, Don César de Santillana, a captain in the cavalry; and the third, his father, is the *alcalde* Don Rodrigo de Santillana. The travelers arrive. Accompanied by the servant, Aurora enters the inn, but her father, Gabriel de Espinosa, has gone to make a call and will come later. Through César's conversation with the servant, who was formerly a soldier serving under his command, it is revealed that the *alcalde* has started a *proceso* against Espinosa for some serious crime and plans to arrest him as he enters the inn. César, although officially aiding his father's investigation, is strangely attracted by Gabriel and wishes to warn him in spite of the servant's advice to avoid involvement with the cold, mysterious *pastelero*. César also seizes the opportunity of declaring his love to Aurora, but she repulses his advances, declaring that she already loves another man. When Gabriel arrives, César attempts to tell him of the danger building up around him, but Gabriel knows about it already. His cold, stubborn rejection of César's friendship and his opposition to César's love for Aurora enrage the young man to the point of drawing his sword, but the impending duel is halted by the appearance of Don Rodrigo and the arrest of Gabriel. By the end of the first act, Gabriel's identification with King Sebastian of Portugal is complete. Gabriel's resemblance to the dead king was hinted earlier, and the sword that he surrenders bears the royal arms of Portugal.

The character of Gabriel, outlined in the first act, gains in strength and complexity during the second act, principally through the mounting conflict between Don Rodrigo and his prisoner. The scene in which Rodrigo first interrogates Gabriel is indeed an effective one. Although Gabriel gives his name as Gabriel de Espinosa and his profession as pastry-maker, Santillana refuses to accept his statements. Gabriel moves to the offensive immediately. Since his identity and social status are unestablished, he refuses to behave like a common prisoner before a judge, and he leads Don Rodrigo through a sit-down-stand-up procedure that destroys the *alcalde*'s arrogant self-confidence. The story of his life which Gabriel tells Don Rodrigo is a romantic yarn filled with half-truths and inferences that increase his listener's uneasiness. When quite young, Gabriel says, he left his unnamed, noble family and became a pirate. After amassing a fortune, he left the sea and fought with the Duke of Alba under an assumed name, later moving in court society until an unexpected blow of fortune stripped him of money and position. After wandering around Europe, he went to Rome to make a full confession to the Pope, who sent him on a pilgrimage to the Holy Land and commanded him to renounce name and family. He then journeyed to Venice, where the state gave him official protection as a pirate. He rescued Aurora, who is not really his daughter, from a Turkish ship. She is now an adopted daughter of the Venetian government and will inherit the fortune he left there. Gabriel ends his long account by refusing to say why he went to Madrigal and why he is going to Portugal:

> Ni sabréis de mí otra cosa,
> ni nadie más de mí sabe;
> sólo Dios tiene la llave
> del corazón de Espinosa;
> Y si más de lo que digo
> saber importa a la ley,
> llevadme a Madrid: el rey
> me conoce, Don Rodrigo.
> (II, vi)

In the second act the character of Don Rodrigo begins to grow in stature, as well. Although Espinosa's majesty and commanding manner disconcert the *alcalde* temporarily, he courageously returns to the attack. Espinosa has shown him three official documents—his discharge from the Duke of Alba, a papal bull of absolution, and the protection of the Venetian government—all bearing names which are admittedly assumed. Don Rodrigo believes that the Marquis of Tavira, who fought with King Sebastian in Africa, can give more reliable testimony about Espinosa's true identity. The marquis is summoned, and Don Rodrigo questions him about Sebastian as Espinosa sits unobserved in the shadow. Dramatic tension mounts as details of the marquis' information match many of those mentioned by Espinosa in his narration; and when Don Rodrigo calls Gabriel forward, the Marquis of Tavira falls to his knees exclaiming, "¡Ese gesto, ese ademán, / esa voz, ese semblante / que no olvidé ni un instante! / Es el rey don Sebastián" (II, vii). But once again Espinosa's calm domination of himself and of those around him

maintains the high level of dramatic suspense. He accuses Don
Rodrigo of staging this little farce and stalks out of the room jeering,
"Traedme otro marqués / como ese: aunque sean doce. / Ni ese san-
dio me conoce, / ni es noble, ni portugués."

In spite of Espinosa's unfaltering *sang-froid* under pressure, he is
not completely cold and mysterious. Toward the end of the second
act, the audience is permitted to penetrate the reserved exterior and
share Gabriel's personal emotions through his love for Aurora. In a
monologue preceding Aurora's arrival, Gabriel gives the first insight
into the motives behind his actions:

> A él solo, sí, desenredar le toca
> la peligrosa red que se me tiende:
> sólo el rey puede descoser mi boca;
> él sólo: si me salva o si me vende,
> él con Dios se verá: no es cuenta mía.
> Yo acepto mi fortuna, tal cual sea
> la que el cielo me de; mas vendrá un día
> en que todo mortal con Dios se vea,
> y en aquel día, en que de Dios espero
> temblar ante el semblante soberano,
> yo, de cetro en lugar, tener prefiero
> una palma de mártir en la mano.
>   (II, xi)

His resignation to what he believes is God's will prompts his rejection of César's offer to help him escape. Aurora, who extends César's
offer, tells Gabriel that she knows he is not her father; but even their
mutual profession of love cannot change his determination:

> tú eres la sola flor que brotar hizo
> en mi camino Dios . . . Dios, que al ponerme
> sobre la tierra, me alfombró de espinas
> la senda que mis pies recorrer deben;
> pero yo no merezco tu amor santo:
> yo soy un árbol, cuyo tronco estéril,
> despojado de vida por el rayo,
> ya ni sombra, ni flor, ni aroma tiene.

. . . .

Mártir me quiere Dios, y obedecerle
es fuerza: vive: y si te dice el mundo
que he sido un impostor, el mundo miente.
Yo no he dicho jamás que era el que buscan,
y a morir me enviarán sin conocerme.

The third act takes place in Don Rodrigo's office in Madrigal. Three months have passed and the *alcalde* awaits César's return from Madrid with Espinosa's sentence. While Gabriel has gone through interrogation and torture with the same cool imperturbability, Santillana is showing signs of emotional and nervous fatigue. He has the disturbing feeling that something unknown and terrible lies behind Espinosa's ironic conversation and eternal sardonic smile. Gabriel, very much aware of Santillana's growing fears, gives one last cruel demonstration of his ability to dominate the *alcalde*:

> GAB: ¿No es verdad que cuando clavo
> mis ojos en vuestro rostro,
> os hielo el alma y os postro
> a mis pies como un esclavo?
> De rodillas, Santillana:
> Vuestra vida está en la mía:
> viviréis más que yo un día;
> si yo muero hoy, vos mañana.
> ROD: ¡Dios me valga!
> (DON RODRIGO *se arrodilla.*)
> GAB: ¡Calla! ¿Y vos
> lo tomáis como os lo digo?
> Si esto es farsa don Rodrigo:
> serenaos, ¡vive Dios!
> ROD: ¿Conque es decir? ...
> GAB: Que divierto
> mi fastidio, Santillana.
> ROD: No haréis lo mismo mañana.
> (*Furioso.*)
> GAB: Ahorcándome hoy, no por cierto.
> (*Con calma.*)

After Don César's arrival with Gabriel's sentence, condemning him as an impostor to be hanged and quartered, the artistic unity of the play suffers somewhat by the necessity of preparing the way toward the identification of Aurora as Don Rodrigo's daughter. Building on the previous hints given about Aurora's background, she reveals the little that she knows about her family, and finally Gabriel reminds Don Rodrigo how the *alcalde* was forcibly married to a noblewoman in Portugal years before. After Gabriel's execution, they open the papers he left which identify Aurora as the offspring of that unfortunate union.

On the other hand, the emotional impact of the final act is greatly strengthened by the subplot. Without the gradual shifting of interest from Gabriel to Aurora, dramatic tension could not be sustained after the pronouncement of Gabriel's sentence. The execution of a political prisoner would be a weak ending to a powerful drama, and even the unsigned paper from Madrid, identifying the victim as King Sebastian of Portugal, could not impart the proper horror to his death. Something more human, more understandable, was needed. This emotional gap is filled by Aurora's dual relationship to judge and victim. Her scornful rejection of her father's love is a satisfying revenge for Gabriel's death, and the emotional impact of the drama continues to the final curtain without faltering.

The characterization of Don Rodrigo gains in interest and sympathy with the denouement. Although he is an arrogant man who may abuse his authority by being excessively rigid in the execution of his duties, he is not entirely odious. He shows that he is determined and courageous in spite of Gabriel's ability to dominate him, and he pursues the mystery of Aurora's origin even though he knows it will have tragic consequences for him. Nor is he lacking in personal honor and integrity, despite his conduct in Portugal. He tries, too late, to stop the execution and save Gabriel. The double realization that he has killed a king and destroyed his daughter's possible love for him incites pity for him as a human being and adds to the tragic effect of the drama.

The characters of Aurora and Don César are truly tragic, also, caught as they are in a web of circumstances over which they have no control. Aurora sees her lover hanged only a few minutes after she believed they were both free and then learns that the executioner is her father. Don César, torn between his love for Aurora and his duty to father and king throughout the play, is frustrated in both emotions when Aurora is identified as his sister and Gabriel as Sebastian of Portugal.

Gabriel is the overwhelming, dominant figure of the entire drama. Without sacrificing any of the mystery and vigorous spirit of the previous *pasteleros,* Zorrilla has succeeded in ennobling and strengthening Gabriel's character by his calm resignation to martyrdom. If Gabriel and Sebastian are to become one single person, this is the only credible motivation that can be ascribed to him. There is nothing cowardly, abject, or resentful in Gabriel's acceptance of death. He goes to the scaffold deliberately and proudly, knowing he could save himself, yet refusing to do so:

> ... Escuchadme: si yo fuera
> el rey don Sebastián, morir debía
> por la quieted del reino, y mi alma entera
> ser mártir a ser rey preferiría.
> Si soy un impostor, y perjudico
> con mi existencia la quietud de España,
> debo morir también: debo una hazaña
> de mi impostura hacer, y sacrifico
> mi vida a sostener esta patraña
> que mi historia desde hoy hará famosa.
> (III, ix)

> No os fatiguéis: empresa es vana.
> Llegó, rey o impostor, mi último día,
> Y moriré cual debo, Santillana.
> Si impostor, con impávida osadía,
> y si rey, con fiereza soberana.
> (III, x)

Zorrilla's Gabriel de Espinosa is without doubt the culminating artistic interpretation of the Pastry-maker of Madrigal. The historical *pastelero* has changed a great deal from the interesting but pitiful rogue whose dramatic talents and aristocratic friends cost him his life. From the anonymous *Historia de Gabriel de Espinosa* he took on added mystery which was increased in the *comedia, El Pastelero de Madrigal*. Still, he was an impostor and a traitor who deserved to die. It was the romantic writers who first made the change in identity from impostor to king. Escosura's *Ni rey ni roque* presents an arrogant, headstrong king who will do anything, even pose as a humble pastry-maker, to combat the tyranny of Philip II, but it was the artistic genius of José Zorrilla that succeeded in fusing the two persons into one. Zorrilla's Gabriel, end product of a long process of metamorphosis from history into legend, is a worthy substitute for Sebastian of Portugal in the minds and emotions of the Spanish-speaking world.

Reference Matter

APPENDIX A

PRINCIPAL SOURCES FOR THE BATTLE OF ALCAZARQUIVIR

The most widely circulated account of the expedition to Africa and the Battle of Alcazarquivir was Franchi Conestagio's *Dell 'Unione del regno de Portogallo alla corona di Castiglia historia* (Genova, 1585). It was a very popular work; editions in French, English, Latin, and Castilian had appeared by 1642. The Spanish translation published in Barcelona, 1610, has been used in this study. The work has been attributed to Juan de Silva by a few bibliographers, but there is little evidence to support that view. Mendonça and Leitam de Andrada say that Conestagio was working in some supervisory capacity at the Lisbon customhouse during the last years of Sebastian's reign; and both Mendonça and San Román, one Portuguese and the other Spanish, refer to him as a foreigner. If Juan de Silva, who held many important governmental posts in Lisbon, had been the real author, surely these other contemporary writers would have been aware of that fact. Although Conestagio's attitudes are overtly pro-Spanish, he states in an introductory paragraph that he is "libre de los afectos que suelen impedir a los escriptores la libertad del dezir, por no ser natural de esta tierra, ni vassallo de Rey ni de Principe alguno" (p. 2).* This could be interpreted as a denial of Spanish nationality, or it could be a reference to his status as a clergyman. He also states that he was an eyewitness to most of the events about which he writes, but Mendonça rejects this claim on the basis that his information is faulty: "... nem ha razão se lhe dè algum credito, pois não se achou presente, em quanto diz errando o nome aos homẽs, & muitas vezes o officio, & quasi sempre os successos ..." (in "Ao leitor ...").* Both Mendonça and Juan de Silva took part in the battle and were captured; therefore, one would expect their accounts to be fairly similar. Nor is it likely that Juan de Silva would be as outspoken

* Translations of starred passages may be found in Appendix B.

144

in his criticism of the Portuguese as was Conestagio. The modern Portuguese historian, José Maria de Queirós Veloso (or Queiroz Velloso), is of the opinion that Juan de Silva served as Conestagio's informant, but this seems to be a hypothesis without foundation.

In *D. Sebastião, 1554–1578,* 3ª ed. (Lisboa, 1945), p. 315, note 28, Queirós Veloso gives further biographical information about Conestagio: after working in Lisbon, he entered the clergy and served as secretary to Cardinal Sforza. Later he was made Bishop of Nardó, and in 1634, a year before his death, became Archbishop of Capua. According to Roger Bigelow Merriman, *The Rise of the Spanish Empire in the Old World and in the New* (New York, 1918–34), IV, 404, Conestagio later became chaplain to Philip III of Spain and Archbishop of Capua, dying in 1639.

Juan de Silva was born in Toledo in 1528 and died in that same city in 1601. He was one of Philip II's most able diplomats, serving as Spanish ambassador to Portugal during Sebastian's reign and on the Council of Portugal after the union of Spain and Portugal. Although Silva was a Spaniard, his mother and his wife were Portuguese noblewomen; and he was permitted to use the Portuguese title, Count of Portalegre, which had belonged previously to his wife's grandfather. Products of Silva's literary efforts are an edition of Diego Hurtado de Mendoza's *Guerra de Granada* and a fine body of letters. His correspondence with Philip II concerning the African expedition is to be found in the *Colección de documentos inéditos para la historia de España* (Madrid, 1842—), XXXIX, 465–574, and XL, 1–114.

The first account of the Battle of Alcazarquivir published in Spain appeared in 1603 in Valladolid; Fray Antonio de San Román [de Ribadeneyra], *Jornada y Muerte del Rey Don Sebastian de Portugal....* In the "Prólogo al Lector," San Román, a Benedictine monk from Palencia, states that he wrote the book to correct the bad reputation given to Sebastian and his Portuguese followers by Conestagio's biased presentation. He does present a vigorous defense of the Portuguese against Conestagio's accusations of cowardice and stupidity; however, in other respects, he shows little sympathy for Sebastian's extravagant plans and the nobles' submission to certain defeat. He makes a strong defense for the motives and actions of Philip II throughout, taking the rather condescending attitude that the poor, confused Portuguese were better off being cared for by the Castilians. Other than this slight change in attitude and the addition of some detail, San Román follows Conestagio's account very closely, even employing some of the same descriptive sentences.

The most ardent apologist for King Sebastian and his Portuguese followers is Jerónimo de Mendonça (or Mendoça), a *fidalgo* from Oporto who accompanied the expedition as one of the *aventureiros*. Mendonça read Conestagio's work and was so enraged by what he considered to be a false account that he wrote *Jornada de Africa*..., published in Lisbon in 1607. This is the first account published in the Iberian Peninsula by an eyewitness. Mendonça's style is unembellished and straightforward, and his earnest, personal presentation has a ring of truth. The book suffers, however, from being a rebuttal of Conestagio's account. If Conestagio errs in being anti-Portuguese, Mendonça goes to the other extreme in defending them.

The second eyewitness account to be published in Lisbon in 1629 bore the title, *Miscellanea do Sitio de N. Sᵃ da Luz do Pedrogão Grande*. Its author, Leitam de Andrada (or Leitão de Andrade), states that he left his studies at Salamanca to join the expeditionary force. During the battle he fought in the third line of the *aventureiros* (he wanted to be in the first line, but it was so crowded that he was pushed back to the third), was wounded and taken prisoner. Other sources indicate that he later spent several years in prison for supporting Dom António's claim to the Portuguese crown (see *História de literatura portuguesa ilustrada,* ed. Albino Forjaz de Sampaio [Lisboa, 1929–32], III, 48). Like Mendonça, whose work he knew and admired, Andrada was moved to write an account of the expedition and battle by the errors spread by Conestagio; but he is not as emotional in his defense of Portuguese honor and courage as was Mendonça. He is quite critical of Sebastian's refusal to take advice, attributing the defeat to the time wasted at Arzila and the march inland. Andrada's account of the expedition is a short one, being only one of the twenty *diálogos* which make up the book. Other chapters treat a variety of subjects: history of the Andrada family, religious experience, legends, pious poems, etc. According to the prologue, Andrada wrote the book in 1622, but it was not published until 1629, the year in which the author died.

Two other eyewitness accounts—one Spanish and the other Portuguese —written even before those of Mendonça and Andrada, were not published in the Iberian Peninsula until the nineteenth century. The manuscript of Fray Luis Nieto's *Relación de las guerras de Berberia y del suceso y muerte del Rey Don Sebastian*..., bears no date, but it must have been written within a year after the Battle of Alcazarquivir. In 1579 a French translation was published in Paris under the title, *Histoire véritable des dernières guerres advenues en Barbarie,* without name of author or translator. This served as a basis for a Latin version, published in Nuremberg in 1581. The original manuscript, found in the National Library of Madrid, was not published until 1891, in *Documentos inéditos*, C, 410–58. Queirós Veloso conjectures (*D. Sebastião*, p. 307, note 24) that the work was probably not published in Spain as originally planned because it casts doubts on Portuguese courage and would not have aided the political ambitions of Philip II; however, Nieto's criticism of the Portuguese is not as severe as Conestagio's. The prime object of Nieto's attack is the deposed shereef, Mohammed, who is given complete responsibility for the expedition's failure. One might conjecture that herein lies the reason for suppressing publication of the work (if censorship was applied); perhaps Philip II believed that the Portuguese should not be allowed to find a scapegoat for the humiliating defeat. Fray Luis Nieto was a Spanish Dominican monk who accompanied the expedition. His manuscript, dedicated to Philip II, is composed of fourteen short chapters: the first six give a family history of the shereefs and the remainder are devoted to the expedition and battle.

The other account was published in 1837 by Alexandre Herculano and A. C. Paiva with the title *Chrónica de El-Rei D. Sebastião* (Lisboa). The author of this chronicle was identified by the editors as Fray Bernardo da Cruz, a member of the Third Order of Saint Francis, who accompanied the expedition as head chaplain (*capelão-mor*) of the armada. However, recent investigations by Queirós Veloso, published in *Estudos Históricos do Século XVI*, Vol. II of *Subsídios para a História Portuguesa* (Lisboa, 1951), reveal new biographical information about Cruz which shows that he could not have written this chronicle. After the Battle of Alcazarquivir, Cruz entered the service of Philip II, working with Cristóbal de Mora to gain support for Philip's claim to the Portuguese throne. He died in Portugal shortly before September 17, 1579. On the basis of internal evidence, the chronicle attributed to Cruz was written between September, 1584, and 1600. Queirós Veloso identifies the author as António de Vaena, basing his opinion on a comparison of the published chronicle with a manuscript bearing Vaena's name.

Another contemporary manuscript which was known by Conestagio is the anonymous "Carta a hum Abbᵉ da Beira em resposta de outra sua em que pedia a hum amigo seu de Lisboa noticias não so da corte, mas do successo del Rey D. Sebastiam," found in the National Library of Lisbon, Secção de Reservados, No. 398, fols. 18–23. It was published by Rodrigo José de Lima Felner in *O Bibliophilo* (Lisboa, 1849), and Queirós Veloso cites a Spanish translation in the National Library of Madrid, *códice* D.68 (*D. Sebastião*, p. 279, note 30, and p. 298, note 8).

These works, written by contemporary observers and eyewitnesses, make up the primary sources for a study of Sebastian's *jornada de Africa* and the Battle of Alcazarquivir. They also form the basis for the chronicles of the seventeenth century, although in many cases these later historians did not name their sources. The remainder of this bibliographical study will deal with the secondary sources frequently cited by modern historians.

Fray Bernardo de Britto was commissioned by Philip III of Spain to write a chronicle of King Sebastian. The manuscript was lost, but part of it is to be found in the Biblioteca da Ajuda, 49.XI.77, under the title, "Copia das Couzas Principaes que Succederão em Portugal em Tempo de El Rey Dom Sebastião." Britto's account of Sebastian's death is identical to that in a short, anonymous manuscript also in the Biblioteca da Ajuda, "Vida de el Rei D. Sebastião," 52X6–156.

The Ajuda Library contains two other incomplete, anonymous manuscripts which were known and used by later historians. Manuscript 49.XI.73, "Chronica do Nacimento, Vida e Morte del Rei Dom Sebastião com a Origem dos Xarifes; Coroação do Cardeal D. Anrrique & Alterações deste Reino," breaks off abruptly in the middle of a chapter after an account of Sebastian's death; but its narrative is resumed by manuscript 49.XI.74, "Chronica del Rey D. Sebastião o Primeiro deste nome Rey de Portugal." Although he gives no source, the eighteenth-century historian, Father José Pereira Baião, copies the account of Sebastian's death from the first fragment almost verbatim in his *Portugal Cuidadoso, e Lastimado com a Vida, e Perda do Senhor Rey Dom Sebastião, o Desejado de Saudosa Memoria* (Lisboa, 1737), pp. 650–51.

Perhaps the most widely known of the seventeenth-century chronicles is *Chrónica do Muito Alto e Muito Esclarecido Principe D. Sebastião, Decimosexto Rey de Portugal* (Lisboa, 1730) by Manuel de Menezes, who in 1618 succeeded Fray Bernardo de Britto as royal chronicler. Doubts about the authenticity of this chronicle, raised by Diogo Barbosa Machado in the eighteenth century, have been dispelled by Queirós Veloso (*Estudos Históricos*, p. 145).

The two Spanish chronicles from this period rely heavily on Conestagio and Mendonça. Antonio de Herrera's *Historia General del Mundo de XVI Años del Tiempo del Señor Rey don Felipe II el Prudente, desde el Año de 1559 hasta el de 1574,* 3 vols. in 2 (Madrid, 1601–12), in spite of the title which refers only to the first of three parts, goes through the year 1598. His relation of the expedition and battle is taken from Conestagio. The account of Juan Bautista de Morales, *Jornada de Africa del Rey Don Sebastian de Portugal* (Sevilla, 1622), shows the influence of

Mendonça in its defense of Sebastian's motives and Portuguese courage.

The three well-known works of the eighteenth century are not reliable, historically speaking, being a mixture of legend and fact, fictitious dialogue and undocumented chronicles. Pereira Baião's *Portugal Cuidadoso* and Barbosa Machado's *Memorias para a historia de Portugal que Comprehendem o Governo del Rey D. Sebastião...*, 4 vols. (Lisboa, 1736–39), are scholarly works which contain the flaws of a period before history had been subjected to scientific methods of investigation and research. The authors are not *sebastianistas*, yet they do use some of the information propagated by the earlier adherents to the Sebastianist cause. The psychological atmosphere in which *sebastianismo* flourished is even more evident in Luis de Torres de Lima's *Avisos do Ceo, Successos de Portugal*, 2 vols. (Lisboa, 1722–23).

The most complete modern work on Sebastian is Queirós Veloso's *D. Sebastião*, a thorough and carefully documented work. This long-lived and prodigious Portuguese historian was a professor at the University of Lisbon until 1950, serving also as director of the Faculdade de Letras and vice-rector of the university. A member of the Academia das Ciências de Lisboa and the Academia Portuguesa de História, Queirós Veloso has published many books and monographs based on research in the archives of the Iberian Peninsula.

Of particular interest to those who do not read Portuguese is E. W. Bovill, *The Battle of Alcazar* (London, 1952). Although Mr. Bovill lists a variety of Portuguese sources in the bibliography, he appears to have relied more heavily on English state documents and Henri de Castries, *Les Sources Inédites de l'Histoire du Maroc*, 18 vols. (Paris, 1905–36). The absence of full documentation is an additional handicap for those who are interested in source material.

APPENDIX B

TRANSLATIONS
OF
QUOTATIONS

19 So the area that we reached was covered with the dead, both men and horses, to such an extent that it was difficult later to enter there on horseback; and in some places the blood was so plentiful that it came up almost to my ankles. And everywhere there were screams and laments, the dead on top of the living and the living on top of the dead, all cut to pieces, Christians and Moors locked in each other's arms, crying and dying, some on top of the artillery, others dragging limbs and entrails, caught under horses or mangled on top of them, and everything was much worse than I can describe to you now because the memory of what I went through grieves me so.

22 . . . even here, if they wanted to see him alive, it would not be because they loved him so but because they would be freed from the inconveniences that his death could bring to them.

24 . . . a sad spectacle . . . all old and crying and the king more so than anyone.

32 . . . brave, tactful, generous, with very courteous manners, admirable qualities for inspiring affinity, maintaining solid friendships, and producing deep dedication.

36 [Henrique] began to govern, always giving indications that he did not consider the king's death certain. And on this issue there existed such different and diverse opinions that very honest men affirmed that the king was alive and in this kingdom, and they gave testimony about when he had been seen. And although it is very easy for the masses to give credence to such things, in this province they have a greater propensity for it than anywhere else in the world.

Page

39 The madness of this land is enough to frighten one and to make him cry. There are here illustrious and highborn ladies who have taken excessive liberties, as if going on pilgrimages in their bereavement, inventing ways to ask God for the lives and liberty of captive husbands and sons, because there is no forbidden devotion that they will not do nor witchcraft that they will not seek out in order to find out what is happening in Africa.

56 From His Majesty's letter you probably understand the state of these affairs. I promise you, on my word, that if the friars had left me alone and had not obstructed me so impertinently, I would now have this matter cleared of doubts and the *vicario* would have told everything there was to tell. But since he felt himself protected and favored by his provincial, he retreated immediately. And I am waiting for His Majesty to take a strong stand on this. And I promise you that if it is not taken, I do not know how we can bring the matter to justice since friars no longer serve any use in the world except to impede justice and to entangle and disguise matters. And from secluded religious men, they have become suspicious, tricky agents, and the courtyard of the *chancillería* is almost as crowded with friars as with laymen. For the love of heaven, order them to quiet down and withdraw because in my opinion this is a very important affair of state since there have never been, either in Portugal or Castile, uprisings or disturbances in which friars have not taken an important part; and, certainly, if it did not seem a lack of devotion on my part, I would say that just as people would become soldiers in the past in order to live with complete liberty, nowadays they become friars. And they have made me so angry now that you must permit me this liberty and forgive me for having gone on at such great length.

56 an honorable and noble man . . . who was a person of greater esteem than his profession indicated and this fact was shown by what he said . . . and in particular he said that he was disguised in that profession because of a misfortune that had happened to him.

59 You have undoubtedly understood and noticed, sir, throughout my life, how lacking I have been in greed and how much more I esteem honor than wealth, and I seek this patrolling by night and laboring by day as everyone knows. And since, according to the indications given by the beginning of this affair, it seems that it might offer me some profit, I beg you not to let me be deprived

Page

of it now by those who are sleeping and wenching while I am patrolling and working. Don't let them subject me to this insult. It is not just for them to give me a coadjutor who will enjoy the fruits of my labors. And I send this letter for the sole purpose of begging you for this, trusting in the favor that you will do me and in the validity of my request. I assure you that this matter has made me more annoyed than I have ever been in my life.

60   it is not right to let him die in despair this way.

60   a highborn man although he tries very hard to play the role of a baker.

61   I should like very much that [Doctor Llano] be commanded immediately to block the word that Doña Ana is spreading about this fellow Espinosa's being King Sebastian because the impression that a judge is authorizing its dissemination can cause great difficulties.

61   . . . as for his person, I believe that under no circumstances can it be said that he is who they say he is. Rather, he is completely the opposite in looks and appearance because this prisoner is a very small man with a thin face and little flesh and has skin, hair, and beard of a very different color. Furthermore, he has a large, noticeable cloud in his right eye and is not the same age. He is very fluent in Castilian, extremely so, without having accent or pronunciation of any other tongue which rarely happens with natives of other kingdoms. And so for these reasons, as well as the fact that he confessed to me time and time again in the course of the conversation I had with him that he was not the one they said he was and that this was the truth . . .

63   . . . since I had received substantiated reports that my cousin, King Sebastian, was not dead and since I had some indication that he was wandering about on pilgrimages, I, moved by pity, prayed that God might reveal to me whether it was true or false. In the meantime, this man named Gabriel de Espinosa came here and disclosed himself as Fray Miguel dos Santos and to me as King Sebastian himself. And he verified his identity with obvious reasons and many personal details by which I was persuaded to believe it, although it is true that other things that I heard about his profession weakened this conviction.

63   . . . and when I asked him why he went about in this way, he told me that he had sworn to do it on the Holy Sepulcher; and when I understood his reasons for wanting to regain his kingdom

before revealing his identity, he always spoke of serving Your Majesty with such affection and without any desire to take from your realm a palm's breadth of territory so that this was the main hook with which he caught me, together with the fact that I considered him the beloved nephew of Your Majesty and thought that Your Majesty would be very happy when he decided to reveal the truth.

64 . . . his coming and the horses were solely for the purpose of seeing me and not for taking me out of the convent as has been said, because the one who entered it unwillingly, only to avoid displeasing Your Majesty, would not leave it against Your Majesty's will, for in this life and the trials and suffering that accompany it, the only relief I have is the belief that I have served Your Majesty and I consider that adequate payment.

64 . . . I beg Your Majesty, in the name of our crucified Jesus Christ, to take pity on me and to see that the honor being destroyed by Your Majesty's ministers belongs to your niece, daughter of that unfortunate father, and to see that my crime was naïveté and that the punishment for it is excessive. If that man is bad or good, have them deal with him accordingly; may Your Majesty not permit that it be paid by this unfortunate woman and this house and so many innocent prisoners who are not to blame.

64 . . . and so I beg you, in the name of everything I can, to declare yourself to Don Rodrigo de Santillán, telling him who you are, since His Majesty and his ministers will be very happy that you are my cousin, King Sebastian. And I trust in the great spirit of Christianity of His Majesty that he will, without other reference, receive you with as much love as if you were his son since you have never tried to offend him nor have you done anything to cause His Majesty not to do what is just. You, sir, owe it to my honor, for it is sad what they have been saying about it just because I wanted to serve, love, and esteem you as my cousin. And being my cousin will be enough for you to come to the aid of my honor which depends only on your declaring who you are.

65 . . . in short, be guided so that, verifying who he is by his low acts and qualities, the plot and the deceit may be undone without leaving room for anyone to say that those fantasies and falsehoods can be considered to be the truth.

65 Since Your Majesty went away, her mother has her brought to the convent almost every day and keeps her all day long. And she

Page

showers her with gifts, in short, as such a mother should treat such a daughter.

65   . . . this name is one of the greatest indications for me that she is her daughter because the prisoner had no reason to use this name nor should he even have known about it, and on this matter he should be questioned.

68   which is strengthened by the good accounts I have received about the virtue and modesty of the aforesaid Doña Ana from everyone, both within and outside the convent . . . so, if there exists in her any malice, it seems to be in small quantity.

69   Doña Ana herself said that she placed her hopes in that kingdom and also her destiny.

70   I, Don Sebastian, by the grace of God King of Portugal, state that I shall receive as my wife the most serene Doña Ana de Austria, daughter of the most serene prince, Don Juan de Austria, inasmuch as I have, for that purpose, dispensation from two high pontifical authorities. [signed] I the King

70   I call this Don Scribbling and not Don Sebastian!

71   it seems that in this matter he is talking like a person without education or experience because such people think that nothing can be done properly without consulting theologians. And he will undoubtedly want to be on the advisory committee, for which, in my opinion, there is no need.

72   You may draw blood that will grieve you, and perhaps some day you would rather have given your own blood instead of having taken it from the veins of others. I would not want this business to cost more blood than that which you intend to draw. But I fear greatly that the prick will be made in Madrigal and the blood will flow in all of Castile and Portugal.

73   . . . I say that it is not instruments of torture that will squeeze this matter and uncover the truth. Rather, I greatly fear that the blood they draw will act as earth to cover it even more . . . but I end by again begging you, a thousand and one times with all possible insistence, to stop and observe that in a matter of this caliber it is more needful to display maturity and tranquility than the spirit of a law officer.

73   he shows that he is a friar and their opinions about governmental matters are normally not very reliable.

74   there is no man known in the entire area more daring and hasty for such things than the aforesaid Fray Antonio.

Page

75   as for the matter of Fray Antonio de Sosa, whom I believe I know, he is very old, even more so than I. I don't know how, considering his age, his handwriting is so good.

77   . . . for holding him as she did in such high esteem, believing that there was no other truth or religion than what he taught and told her, it is not surprising that he should deceive her with such lies to which she was predisposed by her sentiments and tenderness. All of this is more than enough reason for her not to have informed Your Majesty as she should. And we should be grateful that he did not deceive her in other matters concerning faith which has been done by other persons of less repute, for which we should thank God heartily.

83   . . . and in this way she asked the aforesaid apostolic judge and me, the aforesaid scribe, for forgiveness, kneeling down and prostrating herself at their feet in the presence of the afore-mentioned congregation of nuns, and the same thing was then done by the prioress and the oldest nuns of the aforesaid convent in the name of the entire congregation, with great feeling and tears.

86   he has understood everything contained in the afore-mentioned memorandum to be contrary to the truth and thus, on his knees, he begged the aforesaid apostolic judge for forgiveness and said that he was ready to give him all possible satisfaction for it.

86   . . . it would be most fitting if it were assigned to another disinterested person who might do it with less commotion and to the greater satisfaction of everyone, so that the truth might be known clearly and openly and so that His Majesty and his ministers might know who has served and still serves them with proper fidelity in order to award praise or punishment.

87   a Portuguese with little education and poor judgment.

89   Doña Ana received this decision harshly at first; afterwards she resigned herself and took it in good spirits, and I trust in God that with such a just punishment she will give a good accounting of herself.

91   Notification   Then immediately, the aforesaid having been seen by the said *alcalde* in the presence of me, the afore-mentioned scribe, he notified the aforesaid Inés Cid once, twice, three times, and all those necessary by law that she should tell the truth about what she knows and about what is occurring in this case with awareness that, if in the said torture an eye should be lost or an arm or a leg should be broken or if she should die as a result, it

Page

shall be her fault, account, and responsibility and not that of the aforesaid *alcalde*. Having heard and understood this, she said that she knows nothing nor has anything more to say than what she has already said and declared. And she gave this as her reply, the above-mentioned men being witnesses.

before me
[signed] Joan López de Victoria

91 Torture   Immediately following, the aforesaid having been seen by the said *alcalde,* he ordered the aforesaid criers of Valladolid, Pedro de Segovia and Juan Sánchez, to exercise their duty and to put the said Inés Cid to torture. She was stripped by them and, clad in a loincloth, fastened to two crossbars by a strap under her arms. One to fifteen turns were given the rack where her arms were fastened during which time she was saying, "Jesus, oh, they are killing me. Our Lady of Songs, Our Lady of Guadalupe, you know the truth that I know no more than what I have said. Mother of God, have pity on me. Mother of God of Consolation, they are killing me. My God, judge, have pity on me for I don't know anything else to say about the predicament I am in. May God be with me, unfortunate creature, filled with sins; You know very well that I have committed many but in this case I have not offended You nor do I know anything more than what I have already said. God help me, they are killing me. What will become of me; I'll die. Oh, traitor, I didn't know about your lies." And when the said *alcalde* saw the afore-mentioned and that she was saying no more than what she had already stated, he had her removed from the said rack and put on the wooden horse where she was placed and the cords and screws were tightened in the accustomed manner. After a few tightening turns were given, she started saying, "Mother of God of the Rosary, I know nothing more than what I have already said. Judge, for the love of God, have them read me what I have stated in my confessions and in the last one that they took from me in this town before Doctor Llano and I will say if I know anything more to tell. The child is my daughter and I gave birth to her where I have stated, and I know nothing more than I have already confessed about the tales and lies of Espinosa or about this matter." When the said judge saw this, he ordered me, the afore-mentioned scribe, to read the aforesaid confessions made by her. And they were read to her by me, the aforesaid scribe. And when they were heard by her, she said that she

Page

has nothing else to say about her present situation other than that which she has stated and declared in the said confessions, all of which is the truth and what she knows about what has happened, upon the oath which she took then and now.... And she stated her age as being that previously stated and did not sign because she did not know how. And the aforesaid *alcalde* signed it with his name.

[signed] Don Rodrigo de Santillán
passed before me
[signed] Joan López de Victoria

93   you Portuguese are so vain that you don't want to acknowledge him because of his dress. Don't be afraid of saying it for no evil will come to you through this; on the contrary, great benefit.

94   Sentence of Espinosa

In the legal proceedings between the prosecutor of His Majesty, the accuser, and Gabriel de Espinosa, prisoner accused by the guilt ascribed to him as a result of the investigation made in this suit, I find that I should and do condemn the said Gabriel de Espinosa to be taken from the prison where he is held, placed in a *serón* (basket-like vehicle), and dragged in the accustomed manner through the accustomed public streets to the square where on a gallows built for this purpose he will be hanged until dead, and, removed from the gallows, to be quartered and the four quarters placed on the roads which will be indicated by me, and his head to be placed in an iron cage and on a pole in the spot indicated by me and by this, my sentence.

95   intelligent and clever ... of great strength and even greater spirit ... [who] had ability and courage for any great deed.

95   Look, Your Grace, I was not born to be a prince or a king but something greater than an emperor because in the midst of my travails I have always been an honorable man.... I am greatly shocked that intelligent people, seeing my qualities, are persuaded that I am of humble birth. Are my characteristics those, by chance, of an ordinary, lowborn man? Would I be so foolish as to undertake such a great enterprise so without basis as they say? My death will disclose who I am and what there is in this. And what I regret more than my death is the damage that will ensue.

95   This gentleman is sent by the king to identify me ... Tell the king how Don Rodrigo is treating his own blood.

Page

96   This is the justice executed by the king our lord and by Don Rodrigo de Santillán in his name on this man for being a traitor to His Majesty and having pretended to be a royal person, being a lowborn and lying man.

96   No such thing.
      God knows the truth.

96   What is this, brother? May Jesus be with the one who loved Him.

96   Ask him for forgiveness.

100   And with this his days were ended and with them this matter which has given so much annoyance to His Majesty, to Your Lordship, and to everyone.

104   . . . beautiful child, so like the nursemaid that it confirmed her being the mother; so that with this was undone all that Espinosa had said about its belonging to a noble lady . . .

      . . . gave birth to a boy, a beautiful child, so like the little girl that although one might wish to, one could not deny that they came from the same mold, with which it was completely established that that woman was the mother of the little girl, and that what Espinosa had said about her being the daughter of a noble lady was false.

109   I have very poor shoulders for heavy loads for I was not born to work for a living.

111   . . . nor does he send anyone to identify him although the prisoner says publicly that the king knows very well who he is and if he does not, let him send someone to identify him for there are plenty of people who can. . . .

111   . . . it cannot be said that the obligation of the vow stopped him, or even less, devotion—that because of devotion alone he should deprive himself of a whole kingdom.

111   . . . it cannot be said that the obligation of the vow stopped him, or even less the devotion toward keeping it, for so much devotion cannot be presumed in a person who was running after a woman of easy virtue in Valladolid—that because of devotion alone he should deprive himself of a whole kingdom.

113   he seems to have spent all his life weaving fabrics similar to that one that he and Fray Miguel were weaving rather than making silk or cloth of other material.

114   to dishonor them, because I don't owe it to them, nor does he who treats me this way.

114   . . . there are considerable indications that he was a person above

Page

the ordinary; the good appearance that he had, his seriousness, and his face were not those of a common person; his verve, intelligence, and bearing in public. The same thing can be said of his knowing so many languages, his excellent horsemanship, and the fact that he was a mounted soldier. About this and his having given very good proof of his strength and valor, there is no doubt.

115   I confess that I already felt great pity and compassion because of the things that I had heard, and they were increased upon seeing him because when I talked to him he was in his shirt sleeves, wearing pantaloons and a very neat velvet doublet with tight-fitting knit hose, with an appearance and such pleasant conversation as if nothing had happened or were about to happen to him, to such a degree that I, being with the guards at that time, expressed the doubt that he was the prisoner; and if they had not told me anything, I would have believed that he was one of the bystanders rather than who he was.

129   . . . he died a criminal's death but with a martyr's spirit.

129   The same narrow, mean, tyrannical policy that never granted the prerogatives of a Prince of Spain to the conqueror of Lepanto . . . that same policy made Doña Ana a nun.

130   Cowardly as his father was brave, cruel as the other was generous, and fanatical as Charles was religious, no crime frightened Philip when it was a matter of his security, his revenge, or the misunderstood interests of his religion.

130   judging mankind by the yardstick of his own character.

134   I studied its history and tradition, I slept and dreamt its action and characters, and when I saw it clearly in my imagination, I began to put it down on paper: and that is my only dramatic work thought out, co-ordinated, and constructed according to artistic rules: its first two acts are masterfully devised, and I am of the opinion that they give my name the right to figure among those of the dramatists of my time.

144   free from the emotions that usually keep writers from speaking openly because of not being a native of this country nor a vassal of any king or prince.

144   . . . nor is there any reason to believe him since he was not present, making errors in everything he says, about the names of the men and often about their positions and almost always about the events.

163   he also wanted to marry for the sake of having an heir, although the doctors feared that he was sterile.

these people and those of Rochelle [Huguenots]. May He permit those who escaped to mend their ways.

169 believing, as did everyone, that King Sebastian was alive and out of respect for him refused to inhabit them.

169 . . . this has as little foundation as other things that are stirred up here . . . it certainly is shocking to see such lack of civilization in such prudent people.

169 was a nobleman (not of the king's household or the court, of course) whose name we do not know nor is it fitting that it be known. . . .

170 that each one in his own house could do what he liked. . . .

171 Portugal, to what depths you have sunk! I am the cause of your misfortune! Unhappy Sebastian, with what penance can you possibly expiate your guilt?

172 really, he has had and still has great credit and authority in that country.
a man of good judgment and important in his order.
such an intelligent and clever man.
of great intelligence, rare prudence, extensive education, and known always as a great clergyman and servant of God.

172 never has there been an evil of any importance or a crime of any seriousness where a converted Jew hasn't played a part.

174 some outgrowth of the seed sown by Fray Miguel and some fraud.

174 it seems more to be a lack of brains on the part of the prisoner at Evora than anything else.

NOTES

Translations of starred passages may be found in Appendix B.

1   The role played by the Jesuits in the formation of Sebastian's character has been the object of sharp attack by many historians. Rebello
da Silva goes so far as to say that Luis Gonçalves deliberately alien-
ated Sebastian from his grandmother so that she could not interfere
with his plans for a holy crusade, that the priest instilled in Sebastian
the idea of purity to the extent that he was afraid to marry, and that
by the use of religious zeal and fantasy, he transformed the young
king into a willing instrument of the Society of Jesus, devoid of all
human emotion except fanaticism and thirst for conquest. See L. A.
Rebello da Silva, *História de Portugal* (Lisboa, 1860–71), I, 4–23.

2   The author of the *Chronica d'el-rei D. Sebastião*, published under
the name of Fray Bernardo da Cruz in *Bibliotheca de Classicos Portuguezes*, Vols. XXXVI, XXXVII (Lisboa, 1903), states in chapter lxxiii that Sebastian was well-formed with no physical defects or
irregularities. E. W. Bovill has apparently utilized this chronicle for
his description of Sebastian in *The Battle of Alcazar* (London, 1952),
p. 9. The description given above is based on the manuscript, "Sinais
com que nasceo el Rey Dom Sebastião," in the National Library of
Lisbon, Secção de Manuscritos, No. 551, f. 69. José Maria de Queirós
Veloso, *D. Sebastião, 1554–1578*, 3ª ed. (Lisboa, 1945), pp. 115–16,
note 48, speaks of another list of Sebastian's physical characteristics,
compiled in late 1599 at the request of Fray Estêvão de Sampaio,
which also indicates that Sebastian's body was asymmetrical.

3   For a comprehensive study of Sebastian's health, see Queirós Veloso,
D. Sebastião, pp. 101–14. Queirós Veloso conjectures that Sebastian's
physical deformities and ill health might have been the natural consequences of inbreeding since he was the product of some six genera-

tions of the intermarriage of first cousins. The only reference to Sebastian's possible impotence in a contemporary chronicle is to be found in Geronimo de Franchi Conestagio, *Historia de la union del reyno de Portugal a la Corona de Castilla* . . . (Barcelona, 1610), p. 11: "desseava tambien casarse por tener heredero, aunque temian los Medicos que fuesse inhabil para la generacion."*

4 Queirós Veloso, *D. Sebastião*, p. 90.

5 *Ibid.*, pp. 115, 207.

6 For a more detailed account of Sebastian's first trip to Africa, see *ibid.*, pp. 194–202, and Fortunato de Almeida, *História de Portugal* (Coimbra, 1922–29), II, 410–11.

7 For the sake of consistency, these English forms of the Moorish names will be used throughout although a bewildering variety of nomenclature exists in source material: shereef is *xerife* or *jerife*; Mulai Mohammed appears as Mulei Mohâmede, Muley Hamet, and Abou-Abd-Allah Mohammed; Abd-el-Malek is Mulei Maluco or Abde Almélique; and Ahmed is called Abu-el-Abbas, Muley Ahmede, and Muley Amet. The above account of conditions in North Africa is based primarily on Fray Luis Nieto, *Relación de las guerras de Berberia y del suceso y muerte del Rey Don Sebastian,* in *Colección de documentos inéditos para la historia de España* (Madrid, 1842—), C, 410–58.

8 Cristóbal de Mora, or Cristóvão de Moura, a Portuguese noble, went to Castile in the service of Doña Juana, Sebastian's mother, and ultimately became one of Philip II's most trusted advisers. For more detailed accounts of the meeting at Guadalupe, see Fray Antonio de San Román [de Ribadeneyra], *Jornada y Muerte del Rey Don Sebastian de Portugal* . . . (Valladolid, 1603), pp. 23–24; Hieronymo de Mendoça [*sic* for Jerónimo de Mendonça], *Jornada de Africa* . . . (Lisboa, 1607), pp. 3–4; Queirós Veloso, *D. Sebastião*, pp. 230–32.

9 San Román, *Jornada y Muerte*, pp. 45–46, defends Philip against the "imaginaciones y sospechas de personas mal intencionadas"* who suggested that Philip's actions were so motivated.

10 Miguel Leitam de Andrada, *Miscellanea do Sitio de N. Sª da Luz do Pedrogão Grande* ([Lisboa], 1629), p. 209.

11 Queirós Veloso, *D. Sebastião*, pp. 263, 286.

12 For a more detailed account of Malek's efforts to avoid armed conflict see unpublished dissertation (U. of New Mexico, 1960) by Mary E. Brooks, "Gabriel de Espinosa, 'El Pastelero de Madrigal,' in History and Literature," pp. 16–18, 27–28.

13 San Román, *Jornada y Muerte*, p. 52, states that the nobles were

equipped like royalty while the common soldiers did not have enough to eat: ". . . y en fin todo su cuydado erã los aparadores de plata, las tiendas y pavellones de rasos, sedas, y brocados, y otras semejantes galas, como si fueran a unas bodas entre amigos y conocidos, y no una guerra tan desygual y peligrosa con los Moros de Africa."* The anonymous writer of the contemporary manuscript, "Carta a hum Abb^e da Beira em resposta de outra sua em que pedia a hum amigo seu de Lisboa noticias não so da corte, mas do successo del Rey D. Sebastiam," National Library of Lisbon, Secção de Reservados, No. 398, f. 19, makes a similar comment: "Vêr a pompa, apparato, matalotagem, trajos d'esta gente, tão improprios do effeito a que iam, que mais pareciam convidados a desposorios, que ministros da milicia . . ."*

14 The number of ships and men given by choniclers varies greatly, from 18,000 to 30,000 men and from 800 to 1,000 ships. The figures given here are those generally accepted by modern historians.

15 The correspondence of Juan de Silva and Philip II during this period contains detailed information about the expedition (*Documentos inéditos,* XXXIX, 465-574; XL, 1-114).

16 Conestagio, *Historia de la union,* p. 21, describes the sailing from Lisbon as a very bad one: ". . . porque entre tanto numero de gente . . . no se viò un solo hombre que se riesse, ni que anduviesse con alegre semblante . . . Avia en el puerto un funestro silencio . . ."* As the armada set sail, the royal galley rammed a Flemish ship and a cannon went off by accident, killing a sailor. Both incidents were taken as omens of impending disaster. Mendonça (*op. cit.,* pp. 13-14), one of the *aventureiros,* gives a very different picture: ". . . cõ grande contẽtamẽto, & alegria de todos . . . sem aver alguem em toda a armada que mostrasse tristeza, ou malenconia com tristes agouros . . ."*

17 For further information on the decision to march to Larache by land and Malek's attempt to negotiate, see Brooks, "Gabriel de Espinosa," pp. 25-28.

18 Figures for the size of the Moorish army range from 15,000 (Antonio de Herrera, *Historia General del Mundo, de XVI Años del Tiempo del Señor Rey don Felipe II el Prudente, desde el Año de 1559 hasta el de 1574* [Madrid, 1601-1612], Pt. II, Bk. IV, Ch. ix, f. 192) to 120,000 (Mendonça, *Jornada de Africa,* p. 27, and "Carta a hum Abbade," f. 21). Queirós Veloso, *D. Sebastião,* p. 329, gives the combined forces of Abd-el-Malek and his brother, Ahmed, as 22,000 horsemen, 5,500 foot soldiers, and 26 pieces of artillery. These figures

refer to soldiers receiving per diem wages and do not include volunteers who arrived after July 24. The figures given for the number of men in the expeditionary force who actually took part in the battle are not as divergent. Most of the chroniclers state that Sebastian's army numbered between 16,000 and 17,000, about 1,500 of whom were mounted.

19 San Román, *Jornada y Muerte*, p. 142, speaks of the young boys as a great handicap during the battle: ". . . avia tantos mancebos que sus padre embiaron a la jornada, que como vierõ el negocio mal parado tan a los primeros encuentros, pensaron que no se avia ya de volver a la batalla. Estos desconcertaron tanto a los otros, que se via pelear de una parte la gente de un esquadron valerosamente, y al mismo tiempo, y en el mismo lugar huyr muchos antes de ser acometidos."*

20 "Cartas del rey D. Sebastian y D. Cristobal de Mora acerca de la expedición de Africa," *Documentos inéditos*, XL, 115–35.

21 According to Cruz, *Chronica d'el-rei D. Sebastião*, ch. lxi, when Malek first thought Sebastian would turn toward Larache, he said, "Já Larache não tem remedio,"* a clear indication that he had no intention of trying to stop them.

22 For a more detailed description of the battle, see Queirós Veloso, *D. Sebastião*, pp. 362–90, or Bovill, *The Battle of Alcazar*, pp. 114–40. Another modern work which has not been consulted for this study but which would be useful to those interested in the military and tactical aspects is Julián Suárez Inclán, *Expedición a Marruecos del Rey Don Sebastián de Portugal* (Madrid, 1894).

23 "Foy esta fogida q̃ os Mouros fizerão de maneira q̃ muitos não pararão senão em Fez & noutros lugares mais lõge ainda, dõde se publicou o vẽcimẽto dos Christãos & no cãpo se ouvio por grãde espaço, vitoria; vitoria . . ." (Mendonça, *Jornada de Africa*, p. 37).*

24 Nieto's description of Ahmed is not a very flattering one: "Porque él es hombre muy para poco, y no aficionado á las cosas de la guerra (que as querían allá los Reyes), sino antes muy femenil y amigo de estar siempre dentro de su casa."* In appearance, he was tall, dark, and thin, "y de muy menos gracias de las que los hombres suelen tener" (*Relación de las guerras*, ch. xiv, in *Documentos inéditos*).*

25 Mendonça's account is followed by Juan Bautista de Morales, *Jornada de Africa del Rey Don Sebastian de Portugal* (Sevilla, 1622), Ch. xxi. This work is also printed in *Colección de libros españoles raros o curiosos* (Madrid, 1889), Vol. XIX.

26 This version is also followed by Herrera, *Historia General*, Pt. II, Bk IV, Ch. xiv. The accounts given by two manuscripts in the Biblio-

teca da Ajuda differ only in saying that Sebastian was first taken prisoner and then killed when other Moors tried to take him from his captors. See Fray Bernardo Britto, "Copia das Couzas Principais que Succederão em Portugal em Tempo de El Rey Dom Sebastião," 49.XI.77, f. 60, and "Vida de el Rei D. Sebastião," 52X6–156.

27 The same account appears, almost verbatim, in the Ajuda manuscript 49.XI.73, f. 147, "Chronica do Nacimento, Vida e Morte del Rei Dom Sebastião com a Origem dos Xarifes; Coroação do Cardeal D. Anrrique & Alterações deste Reino," and in Padre Jozé Pereira Bayão, *Portugal Cuidadoso, e Lastimado com a Vida, e Perda do Senhor Rey Dom Sebastião, o Desejado de Saudosa Memoria* (Lisboa, 1737), pp. 646, 650–51.

28 Both Jerónimo de Mendonça (*op. cit.*, p. 62) and Leitam de Andrada (*op. cit.*, pp. 196–97) were prisoners after the battle and witnessed the identification.

29 A second set of funeral services was held in Belém, September 19 and 20, 1587. According to a *memorial* written by Fray Juan de San Gerónimo, chaplain to Philip II and archivist of the Escorial Library, Philip II received word of Sebastian's death on August 13. See "Nueva que vino al rey don Felippe nuestro señor de la muerte del rey de Portugal con su ejército," in *Memorias de Fray Juan de San Gerónimo* (*Documentos inéditos*, VII, 229–34).

30 *Documentos inéditos*, XL, 136–40.

31 Letter from Juan de Silva to Philip II dated December 11, 1578, *Documentos inéditos*, XL, 91–92. On pp. 93–94 is reproduced the *auto* drawn up when Fray Roque received Sebastian's body in Ceuta.

CHAPTER II

1 Letter to Philip II, September 2, 1578, in *Colección de documentos inéditos para la historia de España* (Madrid, 1842–), XL, 141–47.

2 For a discussion of the discovery of this secret correspondence, see José Maria de Queirós Veloso, *O Reinado do Cardeal D. Henrique: A Perda da Independência, Vol. I* (Lisboa, 1946), pp. 61–62.

3 Henrique's position—that of having to choose between certain war and certain absorption by Castile—is frequently stated by Queirós Veloso in *O Reinado do Cardeal*. This is a scholarly and detailed study of Henrique's short reign, well documented with diplomatic papers, personal correspondence, and official records found in Spanish and Portuguese archives.

4 For a more detailed description of António's efforts to establish a legitimate claim to the throne, see Queirós Veloso, *O Reinado do Cardeal,* pp. 211–43.

5 José de Castro gives an accurate and unbiased study of Henrique's marriage plans, based on documents found in the secret archives of the Vatican, in *D. Sebastião e D. Henrique* (Lisboa, 1942), Chs. vii and ix.

6 Queirós Veloso, *O Reinado do Cardeal,* p. 215.

7 Interesting and conflicting evaluations of Henrique's actions can be found in Fortunato de Almeida, *História de Portugal* (Coimbra, 1922–29), II, 460; L. A. Rebello da Silva, *História de Portugal* (Lisboa, 1860–71), I, 534–38, and II, 5–12; Queirós Veloso, *O Reinado do Cardeal,* p. 404.

8 José Maria de Queirós Veloso, "Primeira parte. História política," in *História de Portugal,* ed. Damião Peres (Barcelos, 1928–37), V, 203. Hereafter this work will be given as Queirós Veloso, "História política," and page numbers will refer to Vol. V. J[oaquim] P[edro] Oliveira Martins, *História de Portugal,* 12ª ed. (Lisboa, 1942), II, 73, n. 2, estimates the total population of Portugal at this time to be less than one million.

9 The sentence of the governors, declaring António in illegal rebellion against his rightful monarch, formed the legal basis for Philip's later persecutions of António (Queirós Veloso, "História política," 220–21). More detailed accounts of the Spanish invasion of the Portuguese mainland may be found in Serafín Estébanez Calderón, *De la conquista y pérdida de Portugal* (Madrid, 1885), II, 1–71; Roger Bigelow Merriman, *The Rise of the Spanish Empire in the Old World and the New* (New York, 1918–34), IV, 356–71; Almeida, *História de Portugal,* IV, 18–31; and Queirós Veloso, "História política," 222–40.

10 Both Cristóbal de Mora and Juan de Silva were given seats on the Council of State while Philip was in Portugal. Mora returned to Spain with Philip to serve on the Council of Portugal in Madrid. After the departure of Cardinal-Archduke Alberto in 1593, Portugal was ruled by a board of governors, one of whom was Juan de Silva. There is a very interesting contemporary account of Philip's stay in Portugal with detailed descriptions of ceremonies, decorations, and people in Isidro Velázquez, *La entrada que en el reino de Portugal hizo la S. C. R. M. de don Philippe, invictissimo Rey de las Españas, segundo deste nombre, primero de Portugal* . . . (s. l., [1583]). The *licencia* for printing the work was granted in Lisbon in 1581.

11 The Braganças were among the first to greet Philip, kiss his hand, and offer him homage when he entered Portugal in December, 1580.

12 John Hawkins and Sir Francis Drake even signed a contract with Dom António's representative (Queirós Veloso, "História política," 245).

13 Particularly under attack are António's unsuccessful negotiations with Philip II before the death of Henrique and with the Duke of Alba before the Battle of Alcântara.

14 Queirós Veloso, "História política," 213–14, 252.

15 Queirós Veloso, *O Reinado do Cardeal,* p. 279.

CHAPTER III

1 Among the most outspoken was the anonymous writer of "Carta a hum Abb^e da Beira em resposta de outra sua em que pedia a hum amigo seu de Lisboa noticias não so da Corte, mas do successo del Rey D. Sebastiam," National Library of Lisbon, Secção de Reservados, No. 398, f. 21: "Toda a pessoa que dixer que viu alguma cousa n'este accidente [the battle], e quizer contar historias e dar relaçao de pessoas particulares, não vos fieis d'ella, nem creais o que diz. E devia de ser levada a S. Lasaro, apartada das gentes; porque o caso foi um raio, e ira de Deus que a todos cegou . . . Judicium Dei! que andava a fidalguia tão avinagrada, e tão esquecidos do que quer dizer fidalgo, e tão lembrados das mercancias, mettidos em trapaças e outras baixezas, e tão largos nas consciencias e soberbos na vida, que se Deus não dera este açoute, pouca differença havia de muitos d'esses aos da Arrochella. Elle permitta que os que escaparam se amendem."* Jerónimo de Mendonça is the only contemporary chronicler who seems reluctant to accept the explanation of divine punishment. He renders lip service to the theory, but his doubts are quite strong. He is much more inclined to attribute the defeat at Alcazarquivir to military reasons. See Hieronymo de Mendoça [*sic*], *Jornada de Africa* . . . (Lisboa, 1607).

2 *Relación de las guerras de Berberia y del suceso y muerte del Rey Don Sebastian. . . ,* in *Colección de documentos inéditos para la historia de España* (Madrid, 1842–), C, 410–58.

3 Fray Bernardo da Cruz, *Chronica d'el-rei D. Sebastião,* in *Bibliotheca de Classicos Portuguezes,* Vols. XXXVI and XXXVII (Lisboa, 1903), Ch. lxxv; Fray Bernardo Britto, "Copia das Couzas Principaes

que Succederão em Portugal em Tempo de El Rey Dom Sebastião," Biblioteca da Ajuda, 49.XI.77, f. 148. Thome Roiz Quaresma, "Memorias Historicas de Portugal dos Reynados de El Rey D. Sebastião do Cardeal Rey D. Henrique, e dos Phelipes," National Library of Lisbon, Secção de Reservados, No. 591, f. 85, states that two groups met in the sky on the day of the Battle of Alcazarquivir.

4 Quaresma, "Memorias," f. 83, and Miguel Leitam de Andrada, *Miscellanea do Sitio de N. Sᵃ da Luz do Pedrogão Grande* ([Lisboa], 1629), pp. 200, 207–9.

5 Letter to Philip II, August 26, 1578, in *Documentos inéditos*, XL, 136–40. Isidro Velázquez, in *La entrada que en el reino de Portugal hizo la S. C. R. M. de don Philippe, invictissimo Rey de las Españas, segundo deste nombre, primero de Portugal* ... (s. l., [1583]), f. 5ᵛ, also states that even after his coronation, Cardinal Henrique did not want to move into the royal palaces, "creyendo como todos ser bivo el Rey don Sebastian, por cuyo respecto no quiso habitallos."*

6 Letters from Mora to Philip II dated September 8 and November 10, *Documentos inéditos*, XL, 148–53, 180–87.

7 ". . . esto tiene tan poco fundamento como otras cosas que aquí se levantan . . . cierto que espanta ver tal barbarismo en gente tan cuerda"* (*ibid.*, letter dated November 10).

8 Jerónimo de Mondonça, who relates the story in full in *Jornada de Africa*, pp. 58–59, does not give the young man's name, saying only that he "era hũ homẽ fidalgo, (não da casa del Rey, nẽ da corte por certo) cujo nome não sabemos, nẽ he bem que se saiba. . . ."*

9 Geronimo de Franchi Conestagio, *Historia de la union del reyno de Portugal a la Corona de Castilla* ... (Barcelona, 1610), pp. 168–70. Conestagio gives no dates for these events, but they must have taken place before 1585, the year in which his book was first published.

10 Teófilo Braga was the first to point out the cultural and ethnological sources for *sebastianismo* in his magnificent study of the Portuguese people, *O Povo portuguez nos seus Costumes, Crenças, e Tradições*, 2 vols. (Lisboa, 1885).

11 José Maria de Queirós Veloso, *D. Sebastião, 1554–1578*, 3ᵃ ed. (Lisboa, 1945), p. 126.

12 Anes' nickname, meaning "prophet," is commonly used as if it were his surname. The most comprehensive work available on Bandarra and the sources of his *trovas* is J. Lúcio de Azevedo, *A Evolução do Sebastianismo*, 2ᵃ ed. (Lisboa, 1947).

13 The *proceso* of Bandarra was published by Teófilo Braga in *História*

de Camões (Oporto, 1873); however, because the work is quite rare today, Azevedo has given extracts from the proceso in *A Evolução do Sebastianismo,* pp. 123–29.

14 Interest in the appearance of a messiah was very widespread among new Christians in Portugal during the first half of the sixteenth century, and it was not uncommon for opportunists to aid the fulfilling of messianic prophecies by presenting themselves as the promised savior. This emotional atmosphere abetted the acceptance and dissemination of *sebastianismo.* For a fuller discussion of the pseudo-messiahs, see Azevedo, *A Evolução do Sebastianismo,* pp. 23–28.

15 Braga, *O Povo portuguez,* II, 245.

16 J[oaquim] P[edro] Oliveira Martins, in *História de Portugal,* 12ª ed. (Lisboa, 1942), II, 77–80, compares *sebastianismo* to the Judaic search for the Messiah, the only difference being that the Portuguese did not deify their king. Instead of attaining the category of a god, Sebastian was changed into a King Arthur-like legend which causes Oliveira Martins to conclude that the dominating element in Portugal is Celtic. The two Portuguese impostors appeared in the heart of the country, the mountain area inhabited by "pure Portuguese." According to Oliveira Martins, these two men were not charlatans or impostors, but represented the actual incarnation of the people's desire for a messiah.

17 The principal sources for the information about the King of Penamacor are Antonio de Herrera, *Historia General del Mundo, de XVI Años del Tiempo del Señor Rey don Felipe II el Prudente, desde el Año de 1559 hasta el de 1574* (Madrid, 1601–1612), Pt. II, Bk. XI, Ch. xvii, and Miguel D'Antas, *Les Faux Don Sébastien* (Paris, 1866), pp. 95–104.

18 The Bishop of Guarda, a member of the Vimioso family, was the protector of Gonçalo Anes in the 1550's and later was a staunch supporter of Dom António. Teófilo Braga (*O Povo portuguez,* II, 245) suggests that it was his influence that caused the nationalist party to use the *trovas* of Bandarra in its fight against Philip II of Spain.

19 In *Avisos do Ceo, Successos de Portugal* (Lisboa, 1722–23), I, 388, Luis de Torres de Lima states that the authorities found the prisoner so amusing that they decided he did not deserve to die. When asked why he had let the people call him "Highness" and why he would not allow heads to be covered in his presence, he answered, "que cada hum em sua casa podia fazer o que quisesse. . . ."*

20 See D'Antas, *Les Faux Don Sébastien,* pp. 105–22, and L. A. Rebello da Silva, *História de Portugal* (Lisboa, 1860–71), III, 100–103.

21 Herrera gives his name as Gonçalvo Alvares (*Historia General*, Pt. II, Bk. XI, Ch. xvii).

22 Torres de Lima, *Avisos do Ceu*, I, 381, gives 1583 as the date.

23 Fortunato de Almeida, *História de Portugal* (Coimbra, 1922–29), IV, 51, supplies his words: "Portugal, a que abismo desceste! Sou eu a causa da tua desgraça! Infeliz Sebastião, com que penitência poderás tu expiar as tuas culpas?"*

24 For a more detailed account of João de Castro's activities, see Azevedo, *A Evolução do Sebastianismo*, pp. 32–44. The most lengthy account of the Marco Tulio impersonation is to be found in D'Antas, *Les Faux Don Sébastien*, p. 261 ff.

25 See above Ch. i, note 2.

26 Azevedo, *A Evolução do Sebastianismo*, p. 42. Azevedo says that Castro died shortly after 1623 (p. 54) while D'Antas states that he was still living in 1628 (*Les Faux Don Sébastien*, p. 437).

The manuscript cited previously in connection with supernatural signs preceding Alcazarquivir, "Memorias" by Quaresma, is a presentation of Tulio as Sebastian. It is a strange mixture of fantasy and fact, legend and history. The first twenty folios treat Sebastian's childhood, reign, and the expedition to Africa, and the last ten folios take him from the battle to the point where the *proceso* was being drawn up in San Lúcar. The whole story of Marco Tulio is not included. Quaresma implies that the man imprisoned in Venice was not Sebastian, but that Sebastian was arrested in Florence under Tulio's name. Philip III was informed that the prisoner was really Sebastian, but he was determined to dishonor his royal cousin. The account ends without any attempt to explain away the testimony given in the San Lúcar *proceso*.

27 In *O Povo portuguez*, II, 241–42, Braga states that the Arthurian legends were revived during the first half of the sixteenth century for other reasons and later, many elements from them were used by the *sebastianistas*. According to Azevedo (*A Evolução do Sebastianismo*, pp. 95–96), the Arthurian theme of the *ilha encoberta* was not applied to Sebastian until the Restoration in 1640.

28 Although it was impossible to canonize Bandarra, his veneration was widespread at this time. The day that João IV was acclaimed King of Portugal, a statue of Bandarra was displayed on the altar of the Lisbon Cathedral as if he were a saint. This was done with the consent of the archbishop, and there was no protest from the Inquisition (Azevedo, p. 75).

29 *Ibid.*, p. 101.

30 The most well-known attack on *sebastianismo* is José Agostinho de Macedo, *Os Sebastianistas* (Lisboa, 1810).

CHAPTER IV

1 The primary source for this chapter is the "Proceso contra Gabriel de Espinosa pastelero de Madrigal y fray Miguel de los Santos religioso agustino," Archivo General de Simancas, Sección del Estado, *legajos* 172 and 173. Since the majority of citations will be made to the *proceso,* only *legajo* (bundle) and folio numbers will be given whenever possible. The account of Espinosa's arrest is taken from Santillán's letter to Philip II, dated October 9, 1594, *leg.* 172, f. 1.

2 Copies of the letters are *leg.* 172, fols. 3 bis, 44, and 100.

3 See Roger Bigelow Merriman, *The Rise of the Spanish Empire in the Old World and in the New* (New York, 1918–34), IV, 415 ff., and Antonio Ballesteros y Beretta, *Historia de España y su influencia en la historia universal* (Barcelona, 1918–36), IV, Pt. 2, 16, 54–58.

4 *Leg.* 173, fols. 246 and 270.

5 José Maria de Queirós Veloso, *O Reinado do Cardeal D. Henrique: A Perda da Independência, Vol. I* (Lisboa, 1946), p. 29.

6 *Leg.* 172, fols. 21 and 112; *leg.* 173, f. 107.

7 *Leg.* 172, f. 242; *leg.* 173, f. 227.

8 *Leg.* 172, f. 21; *leg.* 173, f. 227. Throughout the *proceso* there are frequent references to Fray Miguel's powerful reputation: "verdaderamente el a tenido y tiene gran credito y autoridad con aquella nacion" (*leg.* 173, f. 136); "hombre grave en su orden y de buena razon" (*leg.* 172, f. 4); "hombre tan ynteligente y mañoso" (*leg.* 173, f. 2); "de gran entendimiento, rara prudencia, muchas letras y conocido siempre por un gran religioso y siervo de Dios" (*leg.* 173, f. 248).*

Biographical information about Fray Miguel's antecedents is scanty and contradictory. Don Rodrigo expressed the belief that Fray Miguel was a *converso,* basing this opinion on the fact that he was from the Algarve and his parents from Xeres de Badajoz, both places being heavily populated by Jewish converts. Furthermore, according to Santillán, Fray Miguel was expert in the Hebrew tongue and the interpretation of revelations and dreams. There is no further evidence to support Don Rodrigo's statement. In all probability, it was conjecture on his part, based largely on the opinion that "jamas uvo en el mundo maldad muy grande ni delito muy grave en que no intervenga algun confeso" (*leg.* 173, f. 133).* According to a manuscript in the National Library of Lisbon, Secção de Reservados, No. 863, f. 587, Fray Miguel was from Santarém, not the Algarve. The manuscript, "Miscellania Curioza de Successos Varios," bound in a volume bearing the title, "Listas dos Autos da Fe," is a copy of incomplete records of Fray Miguel's execution.

9   Opinion expressed in a letter to the prior of the monastery at Medina del Campo, November 19, *leg.* 172, f. 192.

10 The ministers consulted by Philip II throughout the investigation of the Madrigal case were Cristóbal de Mora and Juan de Idiáquez. Martín de Idiáquez, secretary to the Council of State, prepared *consultas* (actually summaries of correspondence coming from the two investigating officers) which were first read by Philip and then were passed on to Don Juan and Don Cristóbal for their consideration. The secretary also served as a channel for consultation between Philip and his two advisers. After all three had read the *consultas* and had made comments and suggestions—in the form of marginal notes, footnotes, or memoranda—Philip would dictate a reply to the investigating officers, directing the manner in which they were to proceed in great detail. Very often the instructions, particularly those concerning re-questioning of prisoners, would consist of a page with questions to be asked in a column on the left; the judge was to note the prisoner's replies in a column on the right and return the sheet to the king. Don Rodrigo de Santillán and Doctor Juan de Llano enjoyed a minimum of freedom in their investigations, and since it was necessary for them to wait for instructions from the king before taking any action, it is small wonder that the case progressed at a very slow pace. Although he was not one of Philip's usual advisers in state affairs, Rodrigo Vázquez de Arce was also consulted from time to time on the judicial aspects of the case. The Council of Castile was the supreme administrative council of juridical matters, and Vázquez, as president of that body, represented the highest civil authority in the investigation of criminal cases and in the implementation of punitive action.

When Cardinal Granville was summoned to Spain in 1579 by Philip II to aid in the annexation of Portugal, the cardinal brought Juan de Idiáquez from the Spanish embassy in Venice. Don Juan became one of Philip's most trusted advisers, serving as secretary of state, and after the cardinal's death in 1586 he became a member of the king's Advisory Junta, being primarily concerned with matters of state. He also sat on the councils of State and War. When Don Juan was appointed to the Advisory Junta, his post of secretary of state was given to his nephew, Martín de Idiáquez. The post of secretary of state was one of great influence. The most important council of the Spanish government was the Council of State; and although the king was technically the president, Philip did not attend the meetings, preferring to learn of the council's deliberations through his secretary. Since all communication was made through him, the secretary was in a position to wield considerable influence if he so desired.

As has been indicated earlier in this work, Cristóbal de Mora performed many delicate diplomatic missions for Philip II in Portugal. After the union of Spain and Portugal, the king rewarded Mora's services with the title of Marquis of Castel-Rodrigo, seeking his advice in personal matters as well as affairs of state. Mora was a member of the Advisory Junta formed in 1586, having the particular duty of advising the king on Portuguese affairs, and was also a member of the councils of State and War. In 1600 he was sent to Portugal as the first viceroy.

11 Doña Juana, illegitimate daughter of Don Juan de Austria and an Italian noblewoman, was in the Convent of Santa Clara in Naples. In 1603 Philip III allowed her to leave the convent and arranged for her marriage to a Sicilian noble.

There is no evidence in support of Doña Ana's belief that she had a brother named Francisco. In early July of 1595 the Archbishop of Evora imprisoned a man who claimed that he was the son of Don Juan de Austria and the Duchess of Nice. The prisoner wrote to Doña Ana, sending, as well, letters to Philip II and other members of the royal family in which he begged for recognition and permission to enter the king's service (*leg.* 173, fols. 403–6). Don Rodrigo, who had intercepted the mail, reported the incident to the king as "algun ramo de la semilla de fray Miguel y algun embuste" (*leg.* 173, f. 182), and Philip agreed that "mas paresce que resulta poco seso del preso de Ebora que otra substancia" (*leg.* 173, f. 350).* Santillán also expressed the opinion that the prisoner of Evora might be one of Espinosa's children whom Fray Miguel was using to represent Doña Ana's brother (*leg.* 173, f. 187). Espinosa admitted that he had other children, but he refused to identify them for fear that they, too, would be prosecuted. The *proceso* records do not indicate what disposition was made of the prisoner of Evora nor do they show that any effort was made to establish his true identity.

12 For a more detailed account of the difficulties between Fray Juan de Benavente and Provincial Goldaraz and the appointment of Fray

Miguel, see unpublished dissertation (New Mexico, 1960) by Mary E. Brooks, "Gabriel de Espinosa, 'El Pastelero de Madrigal,' in History and Literature," pp. 121–123, 156 ff.

13 Information given to Juan de Llano, December 1, *leg.* 172, f. 75, and memorandum written to Santillán, December 29, *leg.* 172, f. 61.

14 João Coutinho, Count of Redondo, was taken prisoner by the Moors in the Battle of Alcazarquivir. After returning to Portugal, he was an active supporter of Dom António, taking part in the defense of Lisbon against the Spanish.

15 Mascarenhas, Count of Santa Cruz, was captured during the Battle of Alcazarquivir and returned to Portugal in time to lead the so-called defense of Setúbal against the Spanish army in 1580. Along with Juan de Silva, Mascarenhas was one of the five governors of Portugal appointed by Philip II in 1593.

16 Távora, first cousin of Cristóbal de Mora, was a great favorite of Sebastian and served as the king's *camareiro-mor,* one of the highest posts of the Portuguese court. He accompanied the expedition to Africa as captain of the regiment of *aventureiros* and was killed during the battle.

17 The account of Espinosa's execution is based on Santillán's letters (*leg.* 173, fols. 187, 190, 192, and 196) and the account sent to Martín de Idiáquez by Father Juan de Fuensalida (*leg.* 173, fols. 193 and 194). Because Santillán was quite ill during August and was not able to send a detailed account of what had happened, Fuensalida offered to do it for him. Don Rodrigo did not see the priest's report, thus he had no opportunity to edit the comments about Espinosa and his mysterious words. Don Martín evidently found Fuensalida's account too biased; he requested a new one from Don Rodrigo.

CHAPTER V

1 Antonio Palau y Dulcet, *Manual del librero hispano-americano* (Barcelona, 1923–27), III, 149, and Pedro Salvá y Mallén, *Catálogo de la Biblioteca de Salvá* (Valencia, 1872), entry No. 3455.

2 Augustin and Aloys de Backer, *Bibliothèque de la Compagnie de Jésus* (Bruxelles, 1891), II, col. 984, list two manuscripts under Fernando de la Cerda, a Spaniard who died in Segovia, May 26, 1605: "Historia del pastelero de Portugal Gabriel de Espinosa," in the National Library of Madrid, and "Historia extraordinaria y verdadera del caso sucedido en la Villa de Madrid con un hombre que se fingió

ser el Rey Don Sebastian de Portugal," in the British Museum. A note on the latter indicates that the manuscript appears to be different from the work printed in Jerez, 1699, under the title *Historia del Pastelero de Madrigal, fingido Rey D. Sebastian.* The information regarding the manuscripts is faulty enough to cast serious doubt on the accuracy of the author's identification. Nevertheless, José Bartolomé Gallardo lists *Historia del Pastelero de Portugal Gabriel de Espinosa* under P. Hernández de la Cerda, Jesuita, in *Ensayo de una biblioteca española de libros raros y curiosos* (Madrid, 1863–89), II 28; and P. Fr. Julián Zarco Cuevas identifies the author of the Escorial manuscript X-IV-2 as P. Fernando de la Cerda, S. J., in *Catálogo de los Manuscritos Castellanos de la Real Biblioteca de el Escorial* (Madrid, 1924–29), III, 150. It is impossible to ascertain whether these two bibliographers were following the *Bibliothèque de la Compagnie* or whether the Backers used the identification made by Gallardo. The first *Bibliothèque des Escrivains de la Compagnie de Jésus* (Liège, 1855–59) does not list Cerda. A later edition put out by Augustin Backer (Liège, 1869–76) has an entry identical to that of Gallardo.

3   The *Historia* says nothing about the jurisdictional disputes between the ecclesiastical and law officers nor does it mention the frictions which developed later around Llano. Both Llano and Santillán are presented impersonally in their roles of investigators. Only Doña Ana, Fray Miguel, and Espinosa are developed as persons: Doña Ana is represented very sympathetically as the innocent victim; Fray Miguel is the clever schemer; Espinosa takes on new depth as the principal character.

4   The preacher that day was not Fray Miguel, but Father Luis Alvares, according to documents found by José Maria de Queirós Veloso, *O Reinado do Cardeal D. Henrique: A Perda da Independência, Vol. I* (Lisboa, 1946), pp. 27–29.

5   This last item can serve as a good example of the manner in which gossip can distort the truth. Although Don Rodrigo and Juan de Llano preserved an outward appearance of great co-operation, neither trusted the other. Llano, in particular, seemed to fear that Don Rodrigo might complain about him to the officials in Madrid, and upon several occasions he collected whatever testimony he could which would discredit Don Rodrigo in the event of an overt quarrel. In one confession that Llano took from Fray Miguel, Fray Miguel stated that Don Rodrigo was working on the assumption that Espinosa was really Sebastian. Santillán had consulted an astrologer in

Medina who told him that Sebastian had not met a violent death, and Fray Miguel talked to the astrologer by order of the *alcalde*. The testimony insinuates that Santillán was trying to force the astrologer and Fray Miguel to corroborate his belief that Espinosa was Sebastian. This was a very clumsy attempt on the part of Llano for it is obvious from the *proceso* documents that Santillán never entertained such an opinion. At any rate, this line of questioning and a word dropped by Llano or his scribe could easily have grown into the story that Espinosa's horoscope indicated that he was a great prince.

CHAPTER VI

1 The earliest reference linking Cuéllar's name to the anonymous *comedia* is in Cayetano Alberto de la Barrera y Leirado's *Catálogo bibliográfico y biográfico del teatro antiguo español desde sus orígenes hasta mediados del siglo XVIII* (Madrid, 1860), pp. 115–16.

2 The accuracy with which the author of the *comedia* follows the *Historia* indicates that he was very familiar with it; however, when he inserts historical details of his own, he falls into error. In Act I, Espinosa's account of the expedition to Africa contains several statements which should have revealed him as an impostor to the Portuguese nobles. He refers to Francisco de Aldana (the Castilian captain) as Juan de Aldana, to António of Portugal as Sebastian's brother instead of his uncle, and to the commander of the fleet as Diego de Mesa when it was Diogo de Sousa.

3 In the "Proceso contra Gabriel de Espinosa pastelero de Madrigal y Fray Miguel de los Santos religioso agustino," Archivo General de Simancas, Sección del Estado, *legajos* 172 and 173, the little girl's name was Clara Eugenia and her mother was Inés. In the *Historia* they are usually referred to as "la niña" and "el ama" but there is one reference to the *ama* as Clara ("Tratado del Suceso del fingido Rey Don Sebastian del qual, hasta oy se supo, que hombre era escrito por un Padre de la Compañía," Z-IV-2, Library of the Escorial, Ch. iii; and *Historia de Gabriel de Espinosa, Pastelero en Madrigal, que fingió ser el rey Don Sebastian de Portugal. y assimismo la de Fray Miguel de los Santos, en el año de 1595* [Jerez, 1683], Ch. ii). Patricio de la Escosura has also used the name Clara for both the little girl and her mother in *Ni rey ni roque. Espisodio histórico del reinado de Felipe II, año de 1595,* 4 tomos en 2 (Madrid, 1835).

4 While never reaching the artistic heights of Larra, Espronceda, or

the Duque de Rivas, Patricio de la Escosura was among the first romantics to experiment with new means of expression in all genres. In 1835 he wrote *El bulto vestido de negro capuz,* one of the first romantic narrative poems based on Spanish legendary literature, and his first play, *La carta del Buen Retiro,* two years later, is a frank effort to revive the theater of the Golden Age. Escosura also indicated an early interest in the historical novel which, largely through the influence of Sir Walter Scott, was being cultivated by Spanish writers of the 1830's. For a fuller discussion of Escosura's role in Spanish letters see P. Francisco Blanco García, *La literatura española en el siglo XIX,* 3ª ed., 3 tomos (Madrid, 1909–12).

5   Although the historical Sebastian I of Portugal did accept Protestants among the foreign troops who accompanied the expeditionary force to Africa, it is unlikely that he would have approved of the tolerance shown by his literary counterpart. In 1572 news of the St. Bartholomew's Day massacre of French Huguenots was celebrated in Lisbon by special religious services expressing approbation, and Sebastian sent a special ambassador to Paris with the specific duty of expressing the Portuguese monarch's pleasure and gratification for a deed well done. See José Maria de Queirós Veloso, *D. Sebastião, 1554–1578,* 3ª ed. (Lisboa, 1945), pp. 177–78.

6   Four editions were consulted for this study: Madrid, [s. a.]; Madrid, 1930; Buenos Aires, 1941; and Madrid, 1952.

Romantic prose fiction enjoyed a revival late in the nineteenth century when the Romantic Movement, in general, had waned. Fernández y González was one of the most prolific and popular writers of historical novels during the decades of the 1860's and 1870's. Financial necessity drove him to sacrifice quality for quantity, and with the help of collaborators he would often be engaged in dictating material for three different novels at the same time. A more complete discussion of Fernández y González' literary production can be found in Blanco García, *La literatura española en el siglo XIX;* J. García Mercadal, *Historia del romanticismo en España* (Barcelona, 1943); Andrés González-Blanco, *Historia de la novela en España desde el romanticismo á nuestros días* (Madrid, 1909); F. Hernández-Girbal, *Una Vida Pintoresca. Manuel Fernández y González. Biografía novelesca* (Madrid, 1931); and E. Allison Peers, *A Short History of the Romantic Movement in Spain* (Liverpool, 1949).

7   José Quevedo, librarian at the Escorial from 1847 to 1852, published in 1845 a rewriting of the Escorial manuscript Z-IV-2, brought up to date in language and made more entertaining by the use of dialogue:

"El Pastelero de Madrigal o el rey fingido," in *Museo de las familias,* III (1845), 27–35, 55–59, 91–96, 105–110.

José Muñoz Maldonado, Conde de Fabraquer, prolific historian of the nineteenth century, has also treated the Madrigal incident in "El fingido rey de Portugal," a chapter in *Causas célebres históricas españolas* (Madrid, 1858), pp. 249–328. Fabraquer is greatly indebted to Quevedo's work, which he acknowledges; but he has enlarged the account by adding a few documents from the *proceso* and a brief historical background of the Portuguese expedition to Africa and the union of Spain and Portugal. The treatment given the *pastelero*'s story, like that of Quevedo, is more novelistic and imaginative than historical. Although no source is acknowledged, the novel by Diego San José, "Gabriel Espinosa, Pastelero de Madrigal," in *Los contemporáneos,* Nos. 309–310 (1914), is a rewriting of Fabraquer's work which does not improve upon its model.

The only appearance of the Spanish *pastelero* in Portuguese romantic literature is a chapter in Camilo Castelo Branco, *As Virtudes antigas* (Lisboa, [1868]), with the title, "A filha do pasteleiro de Madrigal." It is a whimsical story in which the author supposedly discovers the last descendant of little Clara Eugenia who was really the daughter of Espinosa and Doña Ana de Austria. The child's nurse had lied during the investigation to save the little girl's life.

8   Francisco de Villegas, *La Gran Comedia del Rey Don Sebastian* in *Parte Diez y Nueve de Comedias Nuevas y Escogidas de los Mejores Ingenios de España* (Madrid, 1663); and Luis Vélez de Guevara, *Comedia Famosa del Rey Don Sebastian* in *Ocho Comedias Desconocidas de Don Guillem de Castro, etc.* (*Collección de autores españoles,* XLVIII [Leipzig, 1887]).

9   José Zorrilla, *Recuerdos del tiempo viejo* (Barcelona, 1880), p. 205.

10 So called by Narciso Alonso Cortés in the "Prólogo" to the *Obras Completas* of José Zorrilla (Valladolid, 1943). The text of *Traidor, inconfeso y mártir* used here is from this work, II, 1530–78. An indispensable tool for any study of Zorrilla's work is Alonso Cortés' *Zorrilla, su vida y sus obras,* 2ª ed. (Valladolid, 1943).

11 Zorrilla, *Recuerdos del tiempo viejo,* p. 202.

BIBLIOGRAPHY

Almeida, Fortunato de. *História de Portugal.* 6 vols. Coimbra, 1922–29.
Alonso Cortés, Narciso. *Zorrilla, su vida y sus obras.* 2ª ed. Valladolid, 1943.
——— (ed.). *Obras completas* of José Zorrilla. 2 tomos. Valladolid, 1943.
Antas, Miguel D'. [See D'Antas Miguel]
Azevedo, J. Lúcio de. *A Evolução de Sebastianismo.* 2ª ed. Lisboa, 1947.
Backer, Augustin de. *Bibliothèque des Escrivains de la Compagnie de Jésus.* Nouvelle ed. refondue, 3 vols. Liège, 1869–76.
Backer, Augustin and Alois de. *Bibliothèque de la Compagnie de Jésus.* 2 vols. Bruxelles, 1891.
———. *Bibliothèque des Ecrivains de la Compagnie de Jésus.* 5 vols. Liège, 1855–59.
Ballesteros y Beretta, Antonio. *Historia de España y su influencia en la historia universal.* 8 tomos. Barcelona, 1918–36.
Barbosa Machado, Diogo. *Memórias para a historia de Portugal que Comprehendem o Governo del Rey D. Sebastião, Unico em o Nome, e Decimo Sexto entra os Monarchas Portuguezes: Do anno de 1554 até o anno de 1561.* 4 vols. Lisboa, 1736–39.
Barrera y Leirado, Cayetano Alberto de la. *Catálogo bibliográfico y biográfico del teatro antiguo español desde sus orígenes hasta mediados del siglo XVIII.* Madrid, 1860.
Blanco García, P. Francisco. *La literatura española en el siglo XIX.* 3ª ed, 3 tomos. Madrid, 1909–12.
Bovill, E. W. *The Battle of Alcazar.* London, 1952.
Braga, Teófilo. *O Povo portuguez nos seus Costumes, Crenças e Tradições.* 2 vols. Lisboa, 1885.
Cañizares, José de. [See *Comedia Famosa.*]

"Cartas del Rey D. Sebastián y de D. Cristóbal de Moura acerca de la expedición de Africa y a los negocios de Portugal, despues de la rota de Alcázarquivir" (*Colección de documentos inéditos para la historia de España,* XL, 115–229). Madrid, 1862.

Castelo Branco, Camilo. *As Virtudes antigas.* Lisboa, [1868].

Castro, P. José de. *Dom Sebastião e Dom Henrique.* Lisboa, 1942.

Colección de documentos inéditos para la historia de España. 112 tomos. Madrid, 1842—.

Comedia Famosa. El Pastelero de Madrigal. De un Ingenio. Valencia, 1765. Other editions are Madrid, [s. a.]; and [Madrid], 1746. (This work has been attributed to José de Cañizares and to Jerónimo Cuéllar.)

Conestagio [Conestaggio], Geronimo de Franchi. *Historia de la union del reyno de Portugal a la Corona de Castillo. Traduzida de lengua italiana en nuestra vulgar Castellana por el Doctor Luys de Bavia . . .* Barcelona, 1610.

"Correspondencia de D. Juan de Silva con Felipe II relativa, en su mayor parte, a la expedición de D. Sebastian al Africa" (*Colección de documentos inéditos para la historia de España,* XXXIX, 465–574; XL, 1–114). Madrid, 1861–62.

"Correspondencia de Felipe II con varias personas, y principalmente con D. Cristóbal de Moura, su embajador en la corte de Lisboa, sobre asuntos concernientes a la sucesión de la corona de Portugal durante el reinado del Cardenal Don Enrique" (*Colección de documentos inéditos para la historia de España,* VI, 23–666). Madrid, 1845.

Cruz, Fr. Bernardo da. *Chrónica d'el-rei D. Sebastião.* Edited by A. Herculano and A. C. Payva. *Bibliotheca de Classicos Portuguezes,* Vols. XXXVI–XXXVII. Lisboa, 1903.

Cuéllar, Jerónimo. [See *Comedia Famosa.*]

D'Antas [Dantas], Miguel. *Les Faux Don Sébastien.* Paris, 1866.

Escosura, Patricio de la. *Ni rey ni roque. Episodio histórico del reinado de Felipe II, año de 1595.* 4 tomos en 2. Madrid, 1835. (Also in *Antologiá de la novele histórica españole (1830–1844).* Madrid, 1963. Pp. 751–881.)

Estébanez Calderón, Serafín. *De la conquista y pérdida de Portugal.* 2 tomos. Madrid, 1885.

Fernández y González, Manuel. *El Pastelero de Madrigal.* 2 tomos. Madrid, 1952. Other editions are Madrid, [s. a.]; Madrid, 1930; and Buenos Aires, 1941.

Forjaz de Sampaio, Albino (director). *História da literatura portuguésa ilustrada.* 3 vols. Lisboa, 1929–32.

Gallardo, Bartolomé José. *Ensayo de una biblioteca española de libros raros y curiosos.* 4 tomos. Madrid, 1863–89.

García, Mercadal, J. *Historia del romanticismo en España.* Barcelona, 1943.

González-Blanco, Andrés. *Historia de la novela en España desde el romanticismo á nuestros días.* Madrid, 1909.

Hernández-Girbal, F. *Una vida pintoresca. Manuel Fernández y González. Biografía novelesca.* Madrid, 1931.

Herrera, Antonio de. *Historia General del Mundo, de XVI Años del Tiempo del Señor Rey don Felipe II el Prudente, desde el Año de 1559 hasta el de 1574.* 3 tomos en 2. Madrid, 1601–12.

Historia de Gabriel de Espinosa, Pastelero en Madrigal, que fingió ser el rey Don Sebastian de Portugal. y assimismo la de Fray Miguel de los Santos, en el año de 1595. [Xerez, 1683].

Leitam de Andrada [Leitão de Andrade], Miguel. *Miscellanea do Sitio de N. Sᵃ da Luz do Pedrogão Grande.* [Lisboa], 1629.

Mendoça [Mendonça], Hieronymo de. *Jornada de Africa, em a qual se responde à Ieronymo Franqui, & outros, & se trata do successo da batalha, cativeiro, & dos que nelle padecerão por não serem Mouros, com outras coisas dignas de notar.* Lisboa, 1607.

Menezes, Manoel de. *Chrónica do Muito Alto e Muito Esclarecido Principe D. Sebastião, Decimosexto Rey de Portugal.* Lisboa, 1730.

Merriman, Roger Bigelow. *The Rise of the Spanish Empire in the Old World and in the New.* 4 vols. New York, 1918–34.

Morales, Juan Bautista de. *Jornada de Africa del Rey Don Sebastian de Portugal.* Sevilla, 1622. (Also in *Colección de libros españoles raros o curiosos,* Vol. XIX. Madrid, 1889.)

[Muñoz Maldonado, José], Conde de Fabraquer. *Causas célebras históricas españolas.* Madrid, 1858.

Nieto, Fray Luis. *Relación de las guerras de Berberia y del suceso y muerte del Ray Don Sebastian (que N. S. haya en su gloria) lo cual sucedió á cuatro de agosto de mil y quinientos y setenta y ocho años (Colección de documentos inéditos para la historia de España,* C, 410–458). Madrid, 1891.

Oliveira Martins, J[oaquim] P[edro]. *História de Portugal.* 12ª ed., 2 vols. Lisboa, 1942.

Palau y Dulcet, Antonio. *Manual del librero hispanoamericano.* 7 tomos. Barcelona, 1923–27.

Peers, E. Allison. *A Short History of the Romantic Movement in Spain.* Liverpool, 1949.

Pereira Bayão, Padre José. *Portugal Cuidadoso, a Lastimado com a Vida, e*

Perda do Senhor Rey Dom Sebastião, o Desejado de Saudosa Memoria. Lisboa, 1737.

Peres, Damião, and Cerdeira, Eleutério (eds.). *História de Portugal.* Edição monumental da Portucalense Editora, 7 vols. in 8. Barcelos, 1928–37.

Pérez-Ménguez. Fidel. D. *Juan de Idiáquez: Embajador y consejero de Felipe II.* San Sebastián, 1934.

Queirós Veloso [Queiroz Velloso], J[osé] M[aria] de. *D. Sebastião, 1554–1578.* 3ª ed. Lisboa, 1945.

———. *Estudios Históricos do Século XVI (Subsídios para a História Portuguesa,* Vol. II). Lisboa, 1951.

———. *O Reinado do Cardeal D. Henrique. A Perda da Independência,* Vol I. Lisboa, 1946.

Quevedo, José. "El Pastelero de Madrigal o el rey fingido," *Museo de las familias,* III (1845), 27–35, 55–59, 91–96, 105–10.

Rebello da Silva, L[uis] A[ugusto]. *História de Portugal.* 5 vols. Lisboa, 1860–71.

Salvá y Mallén, Pedro. *Catálogo de la Biblioteca de Salvá.* 2 tomos. Valencia, 1872.

Sánchez Alonzo, Benito. *Fuentes de la historia española e hispanoamericana.* 3ª ed., 3 tomos. Madrid, 1952.

San Geronimo, Fray Juan de. "Nueva que vino al rey don Filippe nuestro señor de la muerte del rey de Portugal con su ejército," in *Memorias de Fray Juan de San Geronimo (Colección de documentos inéditos para la historia de España,* VII, 229–234). Madrid, 1845.

San José, Diego. "Gabriel Espinosa, Pastelero en Madrigal," *Los contemporáneos,* Nos. 309 and 310 (1914).

San Román [de Ribadeneyra], Fr. Antonio de. *Jornada y Muerte del Rey Don Sebastian de Portugal, Sacada de las Obras del Franchi, Ciudadano de Genova, y de Otros Muchos Papeles Autenticos.* Valladolid, 1603.

Ticknor, George. *History of Spanish Literature.* 4th American ed., 3 vols. Boston, 1872.

Torres de Lima, Luis de. *Avisos do Ceo, Successos de Portugal.* 2 vols. Lisboa, 1722–23.

Velázquez, Isidro. *La entrada que en el reino de Portugal hizo la S. C. R. M. de don Philippe, invictissimo Rey de las Españas, segundo deste nombre, primero de Portugal* . . . s. l., [1583].

Vélez de Guevara, Luis. *Comedia Famosa del Ray Don Sebastian* in *Ocho Comedias Desconocidas de Don Guillem de Castro, etc. (Colección de autores españoles,* Vol. XLVIII). Leipzig, 1887.

184   *Bibliography*

Villegas, Francisco de. *La Gran Comedia del Rey Don Sebastian* in *Parte Diez y Nueve de Comedias Nuevas y Escogidas de los Mejores Ingenios de España*. Madrid, 1663.
Zarco Cuevas, Julián. *Catálogo de las Manuscritos Castellanos de la Real Biblioteca de el Escorial*. 3 tomos. Madrid, 1924–29.
Zorrilla, José. *Obras completas*. Ordenación, prólogo y notas de Narciso Alonso Cortés. 2 tomos. Valladolid, 1943.
———. *Recuerdos del tiempo viejo*. Barcelona, 1880.

UNPUBLISHED MATERIAL

Britto, Fr. Bernardo. "Copia das Couzas Principais que succederão em Portugal em Tempo de El Rey Dom Sebastião," Biblioteca da Ajuda, 49.XI.77.
Brooks, Mary Elizabeth. "Gabriel de Espinosa, 'El Pastelero de Madrigal,' in History and Literature." Unpublished Ph.D. dissertation, University of New Mexico, 1960.
"Carta a hum Abbᵉ da Beira em resposta de outra sua em que pedia a hum amigo seu de Lisboa noticias não so da corte, mas do successo del Rey D. Sebastiam," Biblioteca Nacional de Lisboa, Secção de Reservados, 398.
"Chronica del Rey D. Sebastião o Primeiro deste nome Rey de Portugal," Biblioteca da Ajuda, 49.XI.74.
"Chronica do Nacimento, Vida e Morte del Rei Dom Sebastião com a Origem dos Xarifes; Coroação do Cardeal D. Anrrique & Alterações deste Reino," Biblioteca da Ajuda, 49.XI.73.
"Miscellania Curioza de Successos Varios: Culpas que o P. Fr. Miguel dos Santos Confessou contra si com dados tormentos que lhe davão, das quais, depois de sentenciado a morte, confessando-se com o P. Fr. Sebastião Brixiano, da Ordem de S. Francisco, o nao quiz absolver sem primeiro se desdizer, como se desdisse. Anno 1595," Biblioteca Nacional de Lisboa, Secção de Reservados, 863.
"El Pastelero de Madrigal, comedia en 5 actos," Colección Sedó (Barcelona).
"Proceso contra Gabriel de Espinosa pastelero de Madrigal y fray Miguel de los Santos religioso agustino," Archivo General de Simancas, Sección del Estado, *legajos* 172 and 173.
Roiz Quaresma, Thome, "Memorias Historicas de Portugal dos Reynados de El Rey D. Sebastião do Cardeal Rey D. Henrique, a dos Phelipes," Biblioteca Nacional de Lisboa, Secção de Reservados, 591.

"Sinais com que nasceo el Rey Dom Sebastião," Biblioteca Nacional de Lisboa, Secção de Manuscritos, 551.

"Tratado del Suceso del fingido Rey Don Sebantian del qual, hasta oy se supo, que hombre era; escrito por un Padre de la Compañia," Real Biblioteca de El Escorial, Z-IV-2.

"Vida de el Rei D. Sebastião," Biblioteca da Ajuda, 52X6–156.

INDEX

Abdallah, Shereef of Fez, 11

Abd-el-Malek. *See* Malek, Shereef of Fez

Afonso, Pero, 42–43

Africa, expedition to, 10–23; preparations for, 10–15; participation of Philip II in, 11–13, 23; popular feeling against, 12–13; forces of, 14–15; delayed at Arzila, 15–16; march overland, 16–18; description of battle, 18–21; news reaches Portugal, 22; ransoming of captives, 22–23, 26; economic effect of, 23, 28; effects of, 34; supernatural phenomena, 35–36; historical sources, 144–49

Ahmed, Shereef of Fez, 11, 18, 19, 21, 22, 23, 164, 165

Alarcão, Martim de, 79

Alba, Duke of, 12, 28, 29, 136, 137

Alberto de Austria, Cardinal-Archduke, 30, 42, 43, 167

Albuquerque, Jorge de, 79

Alcântara, Battle of, 29, 44, 54, 168

Alcazarquivir, Battle of: effects of, 34; divine punishment as interpretation of, 34–35; evil omens, 35–36; mentioned, 17, 33, 36, 38, 39, 41, 45, 55, 69, 92, 113, 128. *See also* Africa, expedition to

Aldana, Francisco de, 17, 18, 177

Alemcastro (Lencastre), Rodrigo de, 79

Alfonso VI, King of Portugal, 49

Almazán, Marquis of, 67

Almeida, Fortunato de, 171

Alvares, Father Luis, 176

Alvares, Mateus, 42–43

Amaral, Belchior do, 22, 36

Ana de Austria, Doña, 51–90; parents, 52; arrest, 54; letters to Philip II, 62, 63–64, 84, 88; victim of Fray Miguel, 62, 68, 77; relations with judges, 62, 83–84; marriage promise, 65, 68–69, 70, 78; sentence, 87–89; made abbess at Burgos, 90; in *Historia de Gabriel de Espinosa*, 106–18; in *El Pastelero de Madrigal (comedia)*, 120, 121, 124; in *Ni rey ni roque*, 129–30; in *Traidor, inconfeso y mártir*, 134. *See also* Francisco, Doña Ana's brother; Evora, prisoner of

Andrada, Miguel Leitam de, 19, 144, 146, 166

Anes, Gonçalo, *O Bandarra*, 35, 39–40, 44, 48, 169, 170, 171

Anjos, Fray Agostinho dos, 87

António, Prior of Crato: governor of Tangier, 10; conflict with Dom